Animal Dot-to-Dot

Book for Kids

Connect the Dot Puzzles for Fun and Learning

Blue Wave Press

Copyright © 2018 by Dylanna Publishing
All rights reserved. This book or any portion thereof
may not be reproduced or used in any manner whatsoever without the express
written permission of the publisher
except for the use of brief quotations in a book review.
First edition: 2019
Photo credits: Shutterstock

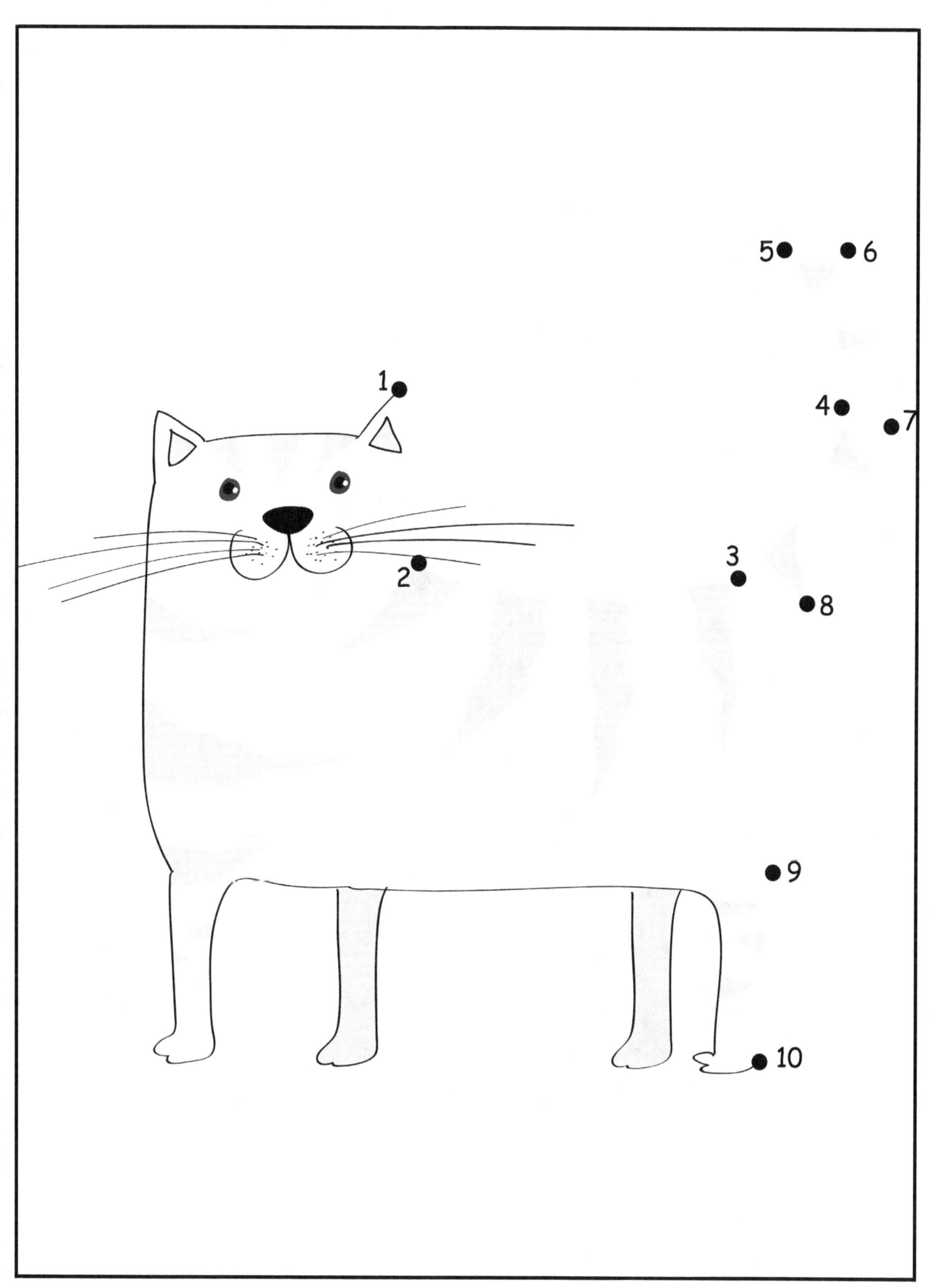

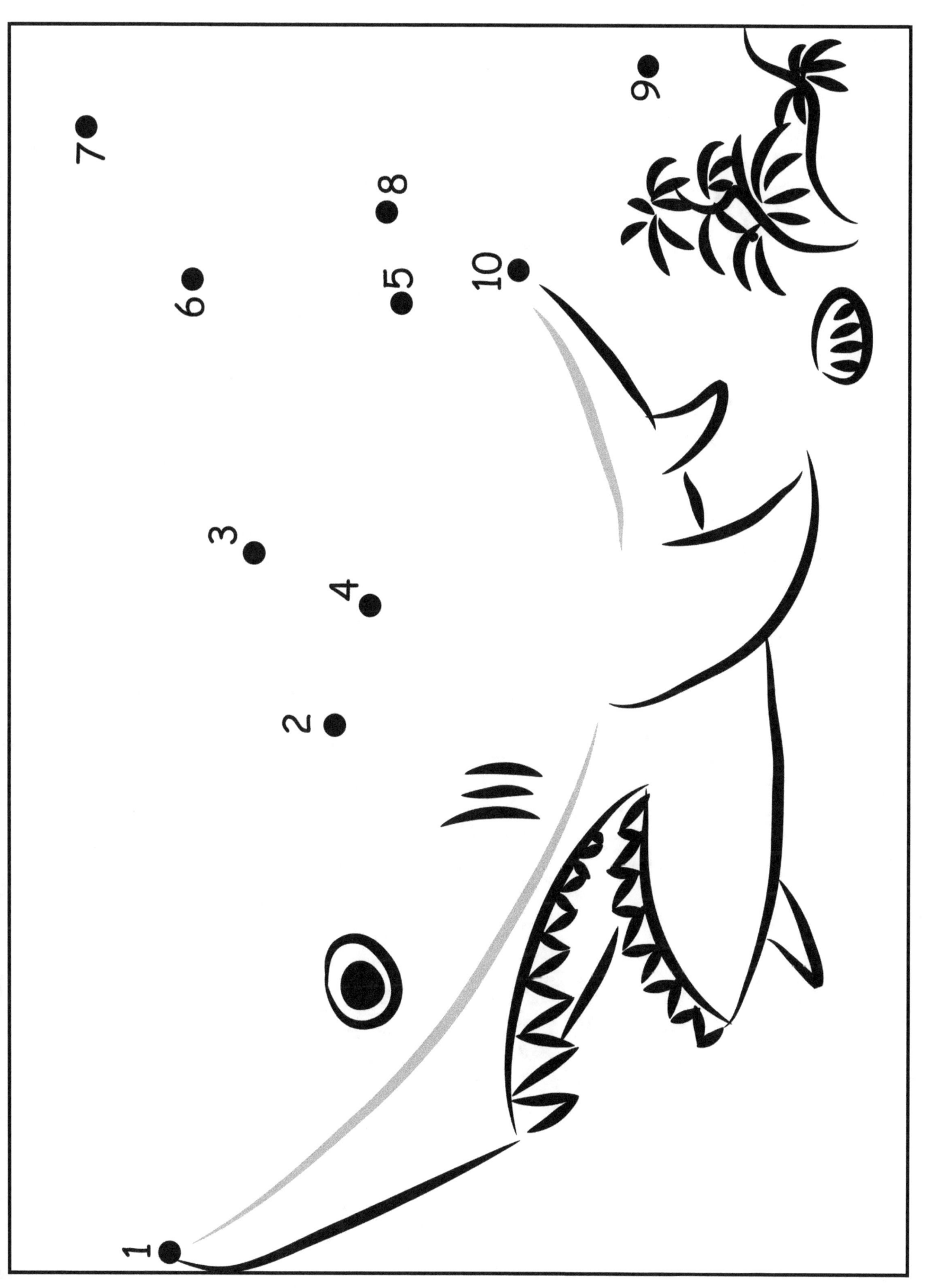

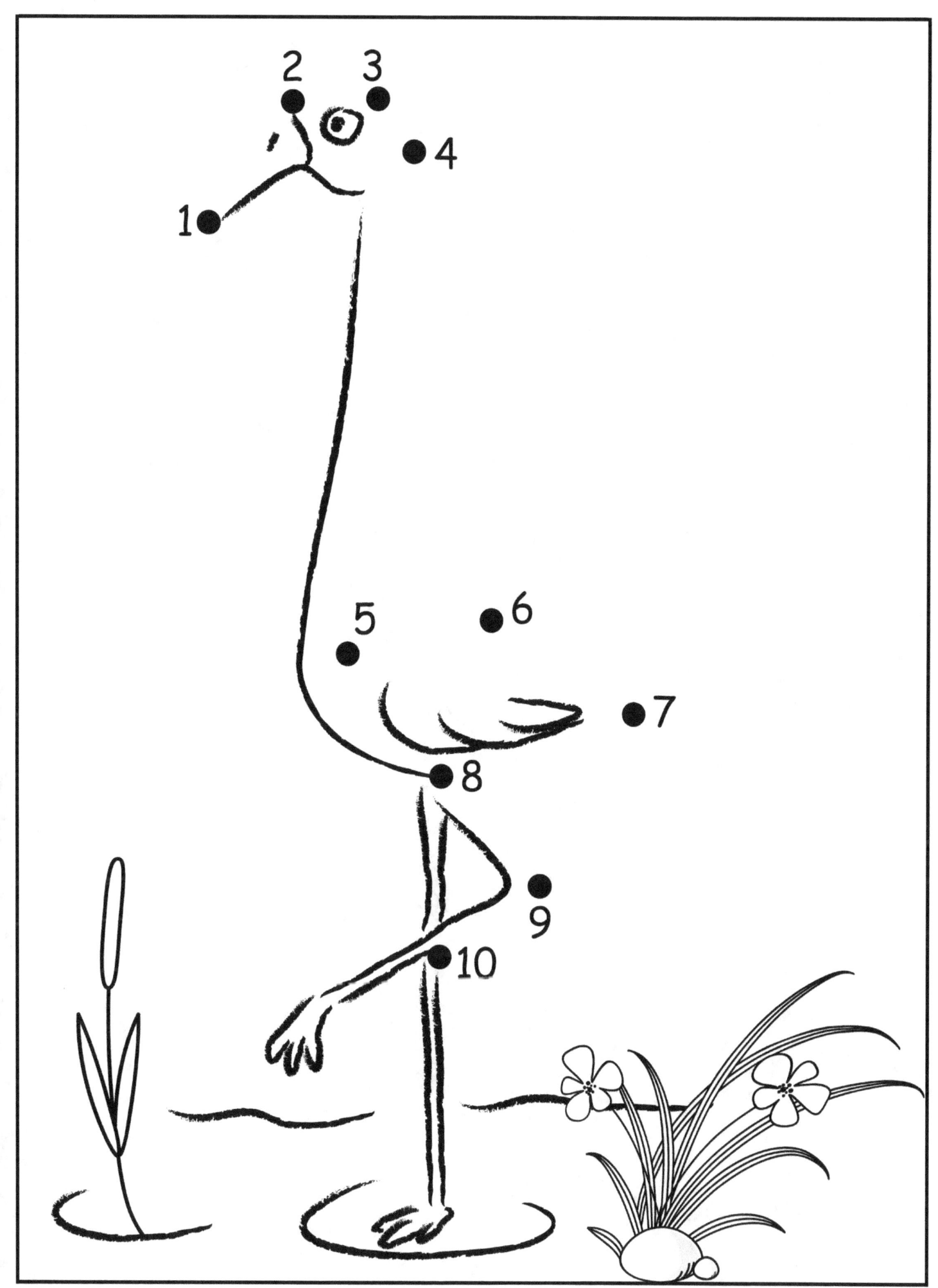

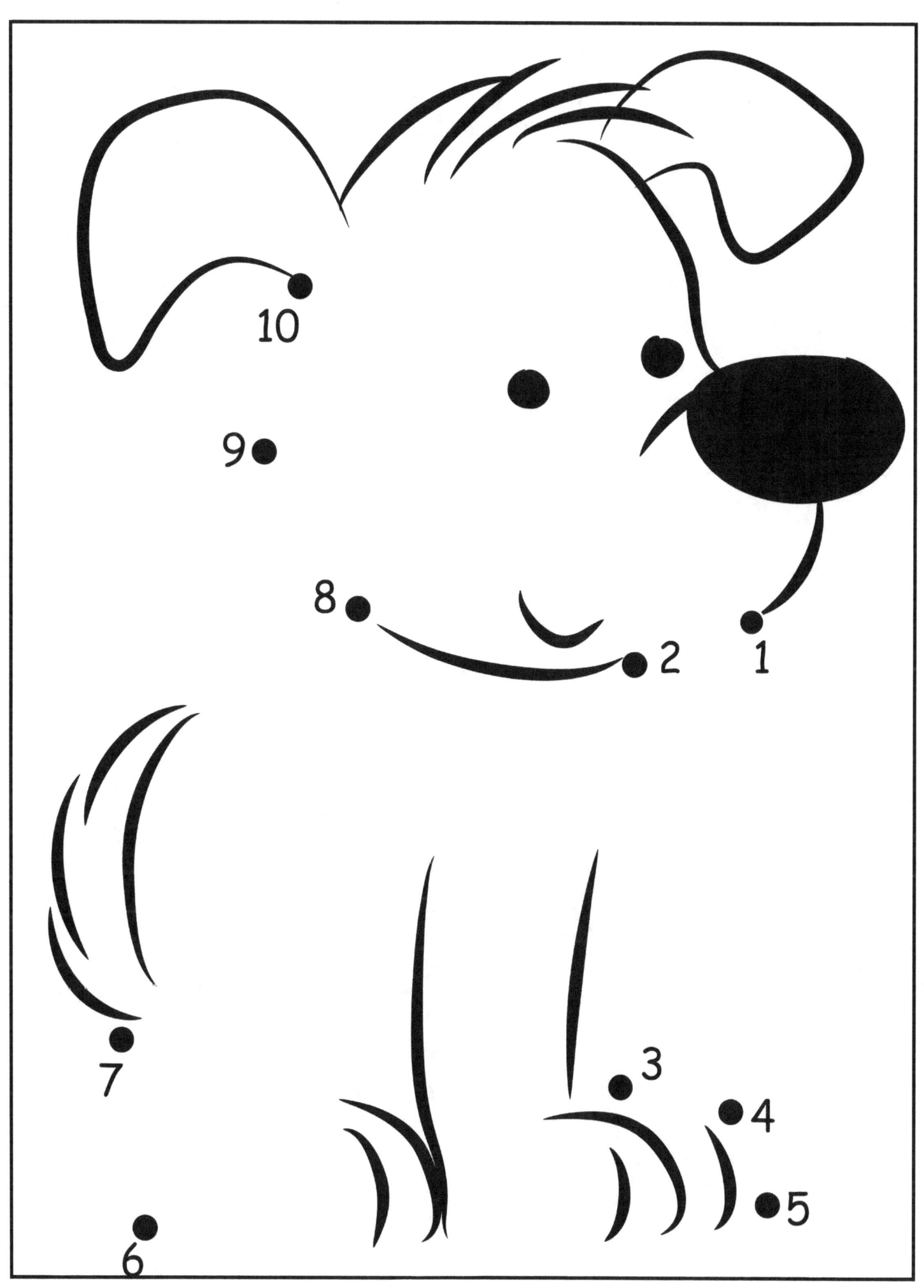

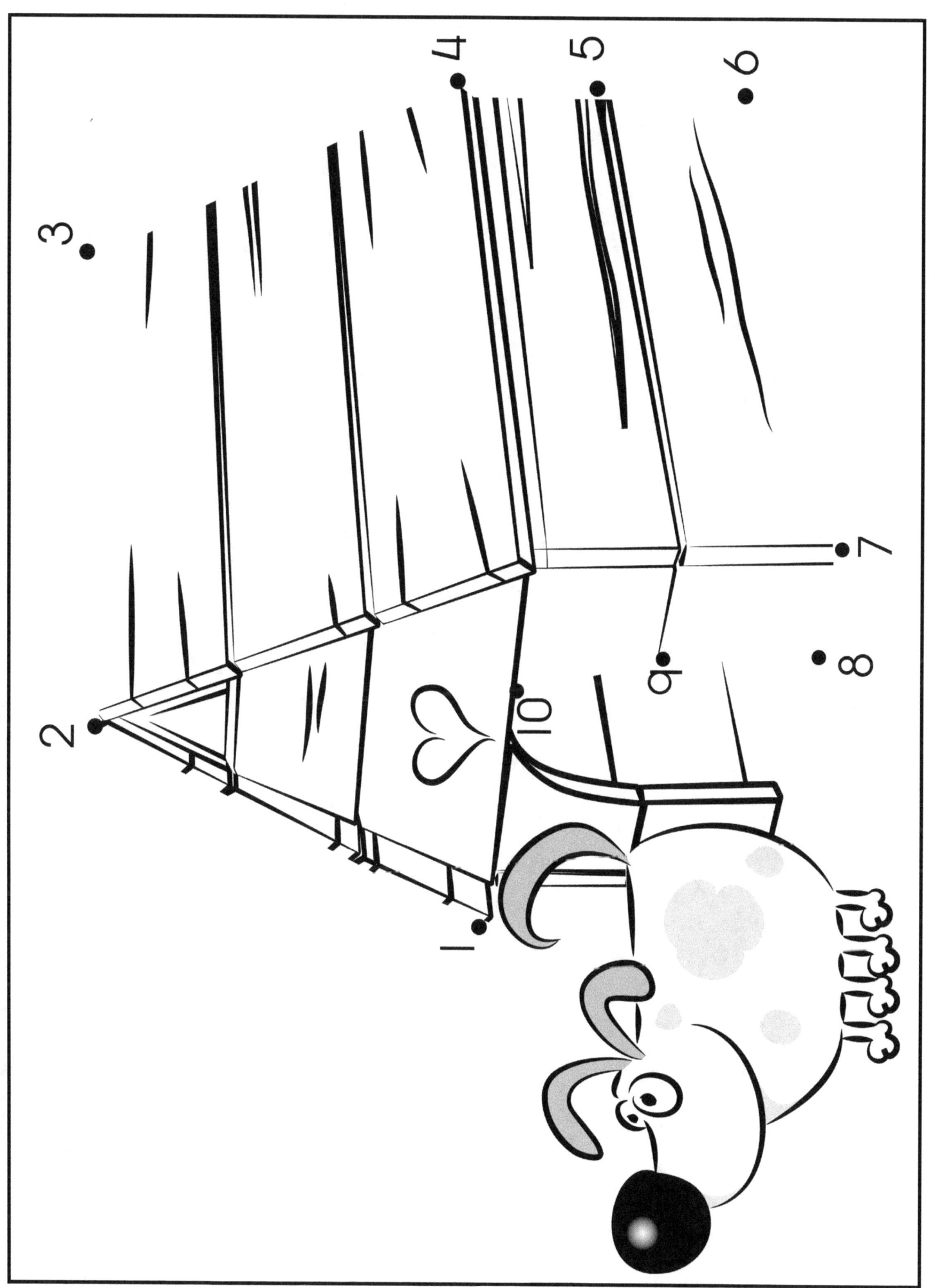

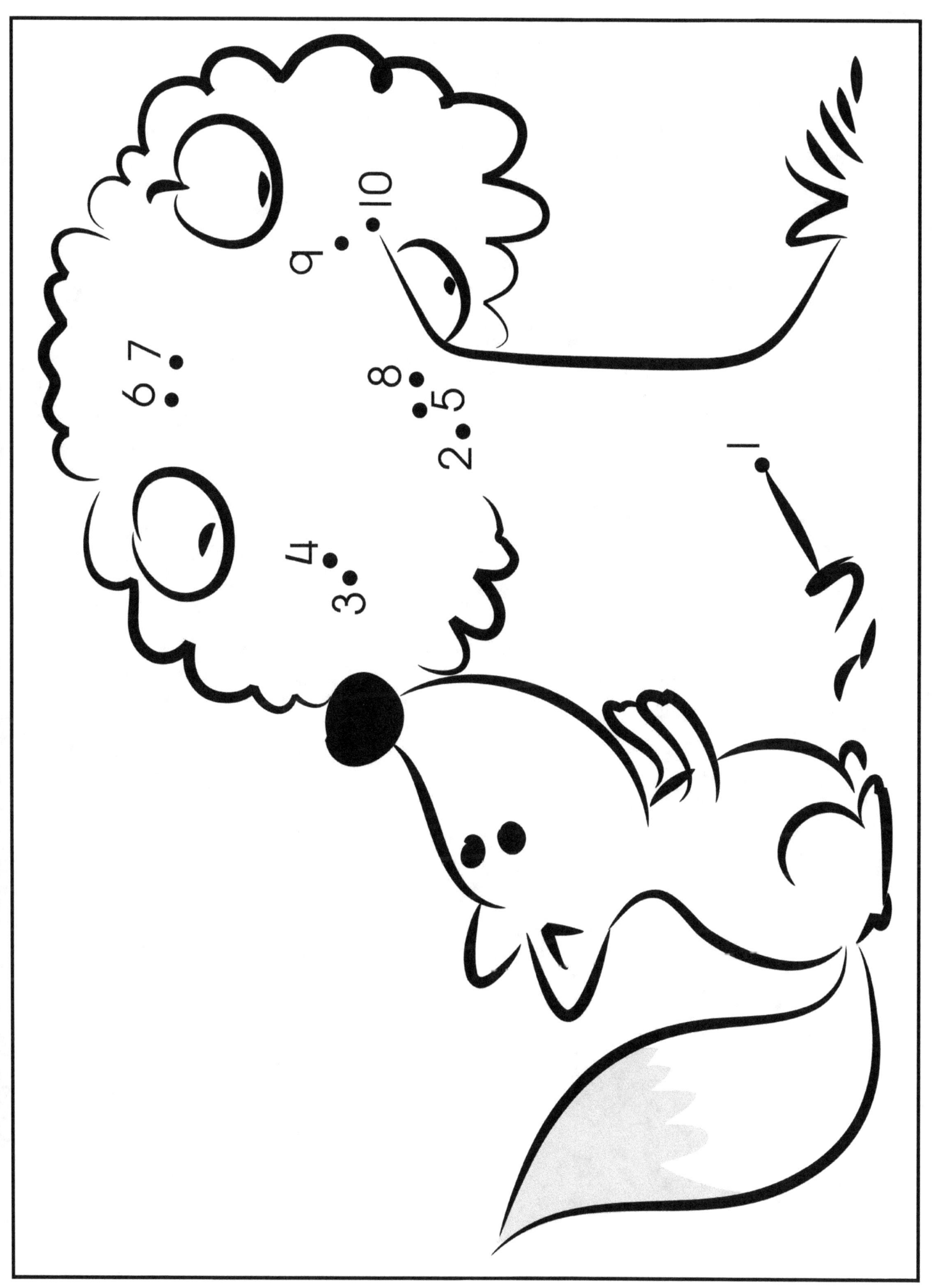

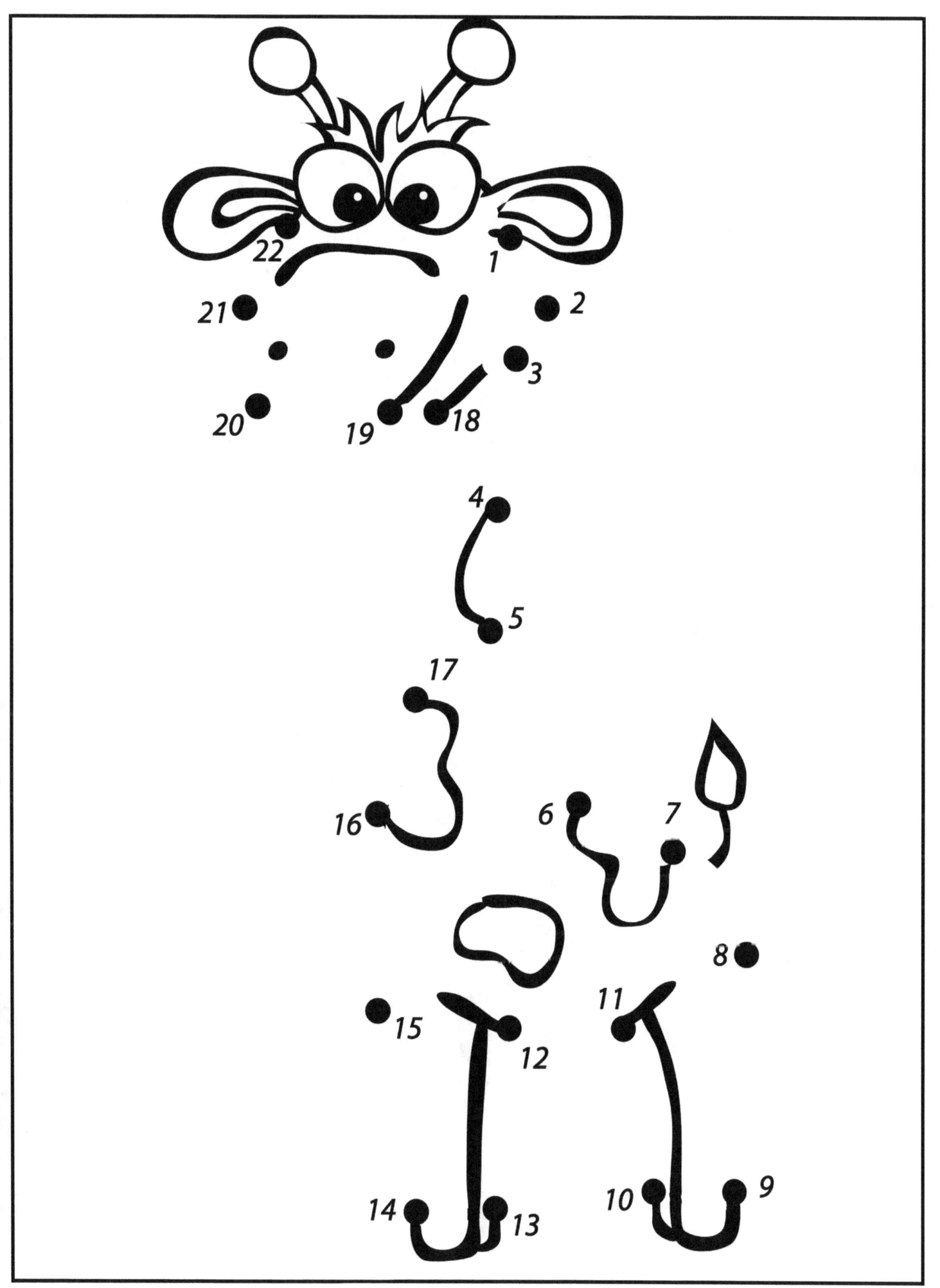

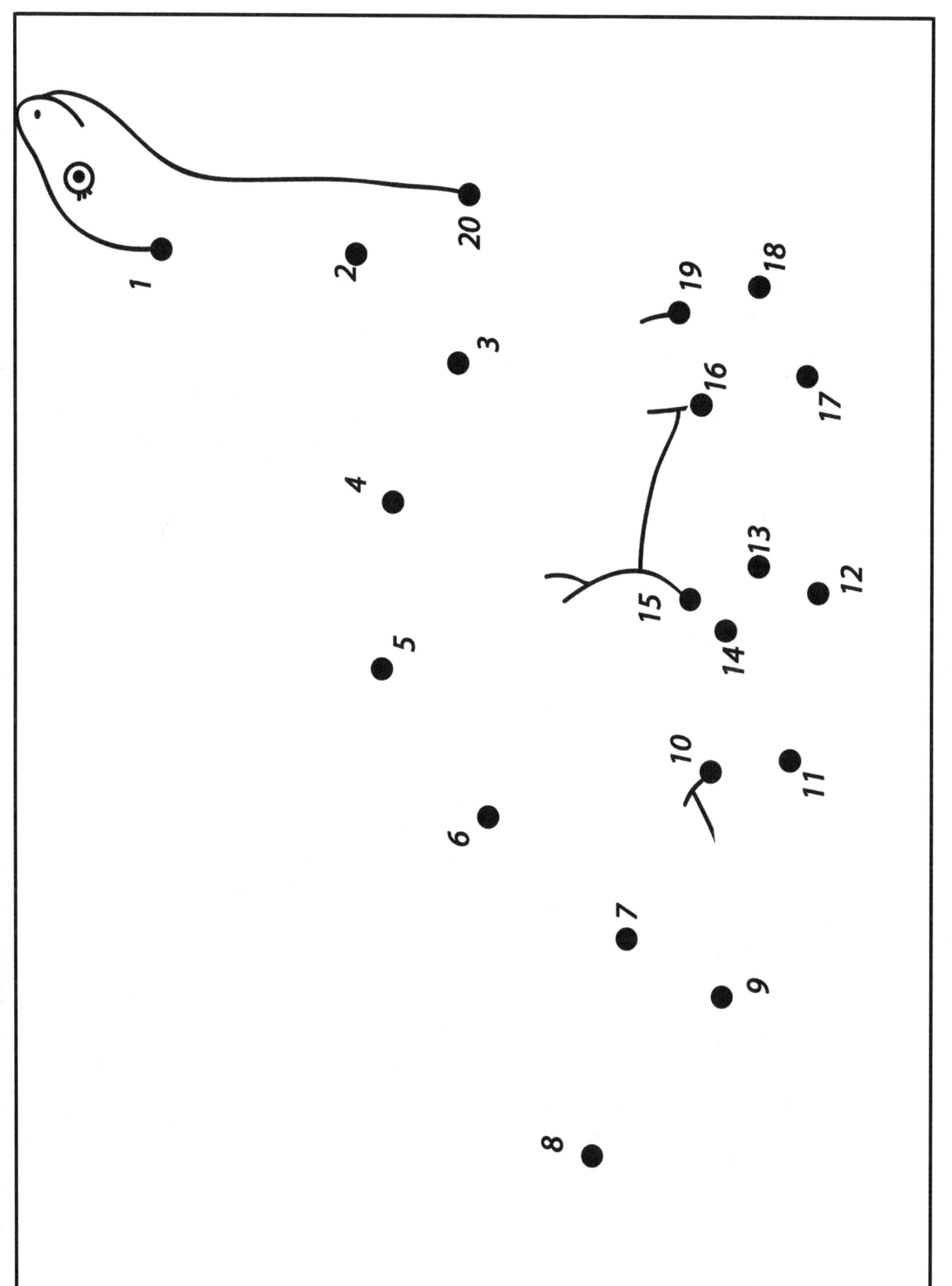

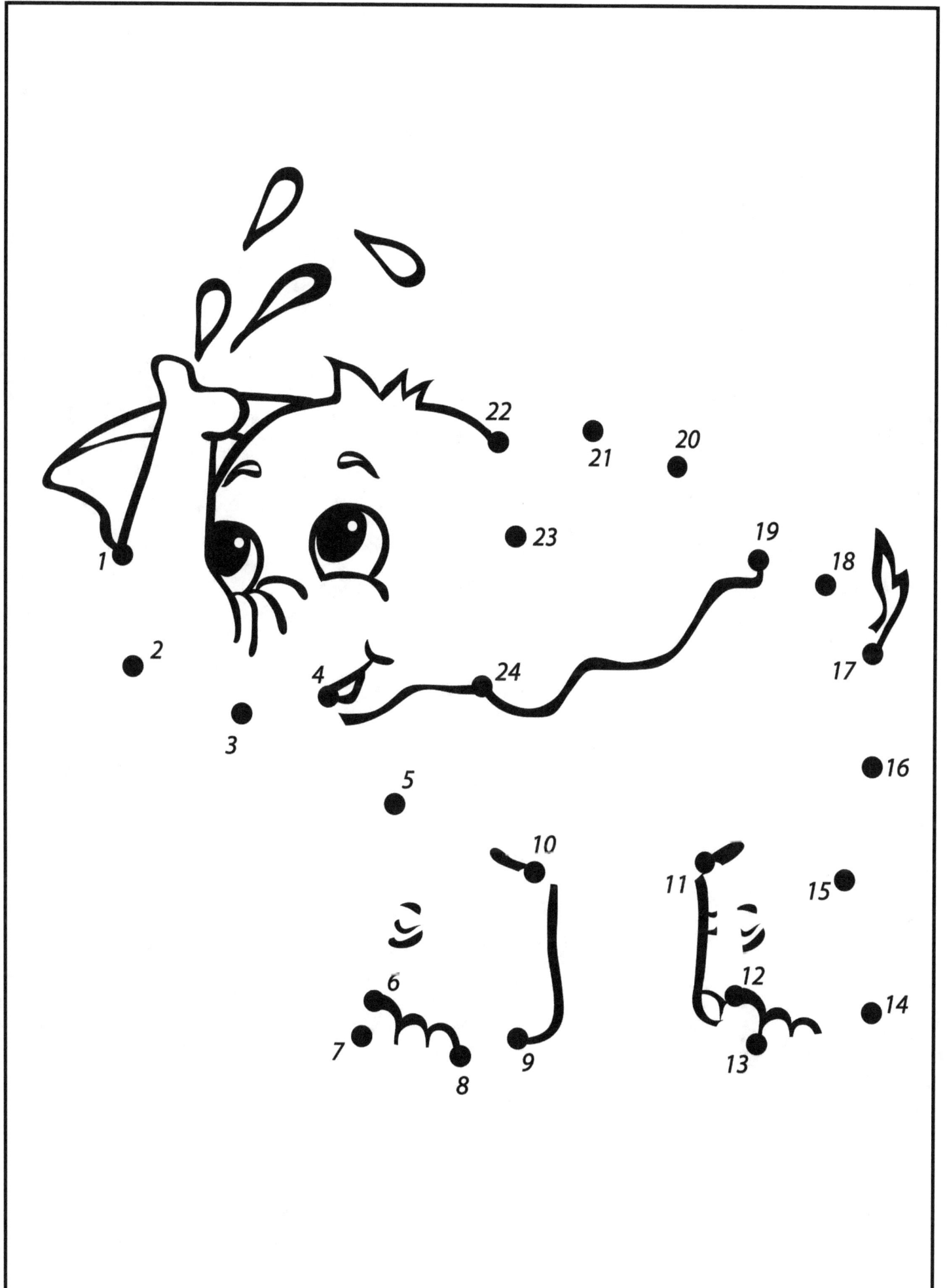

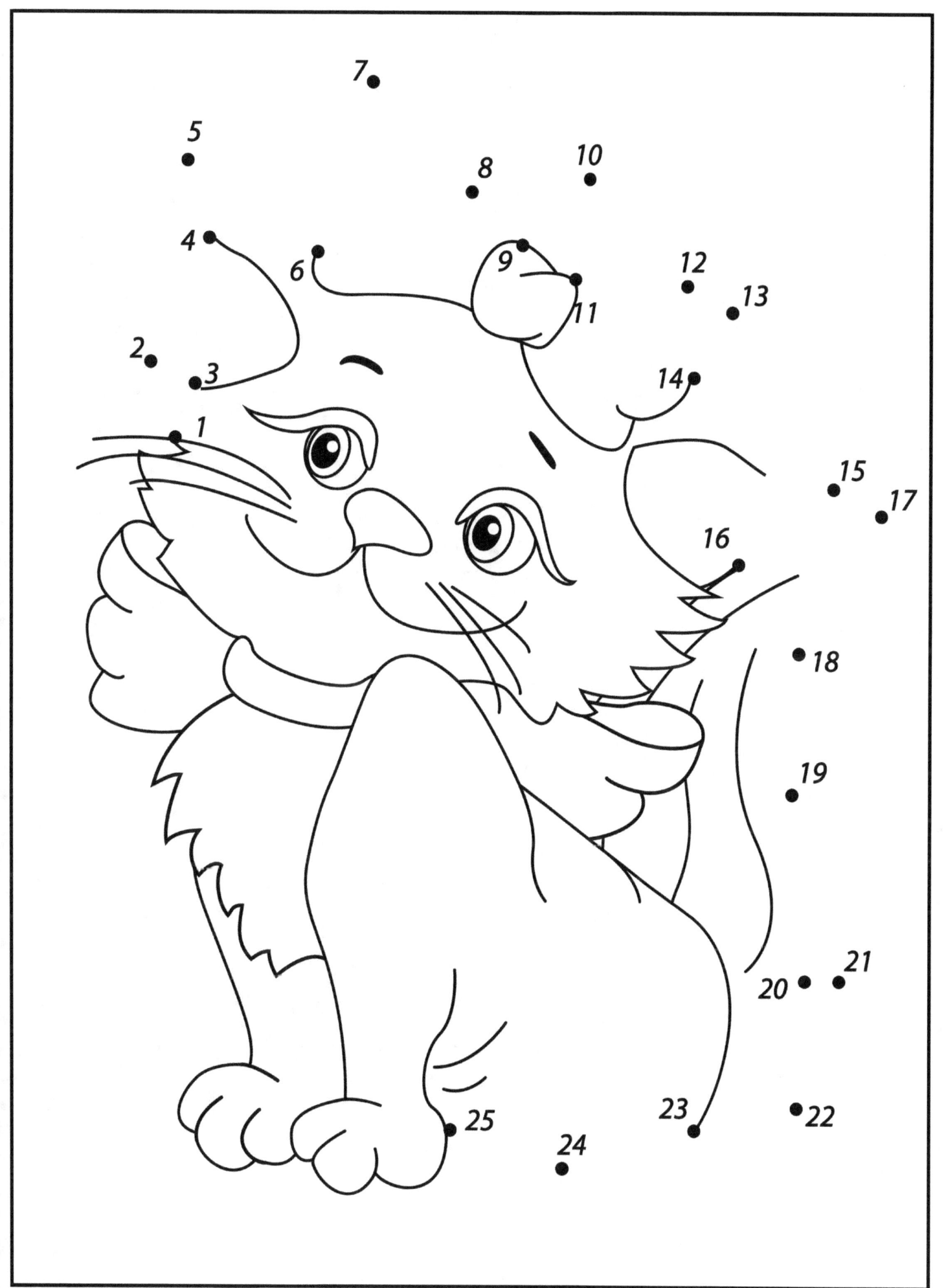

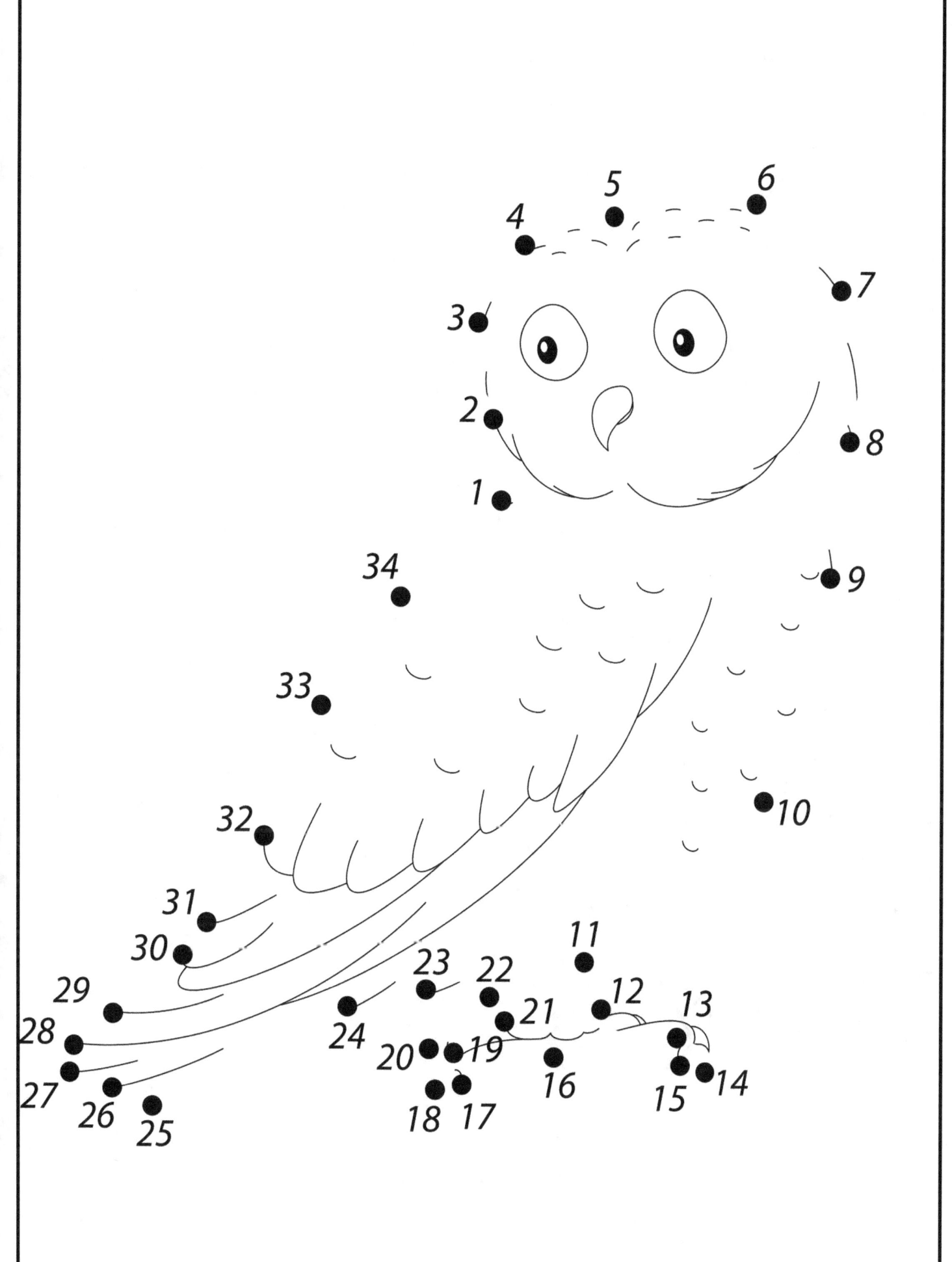

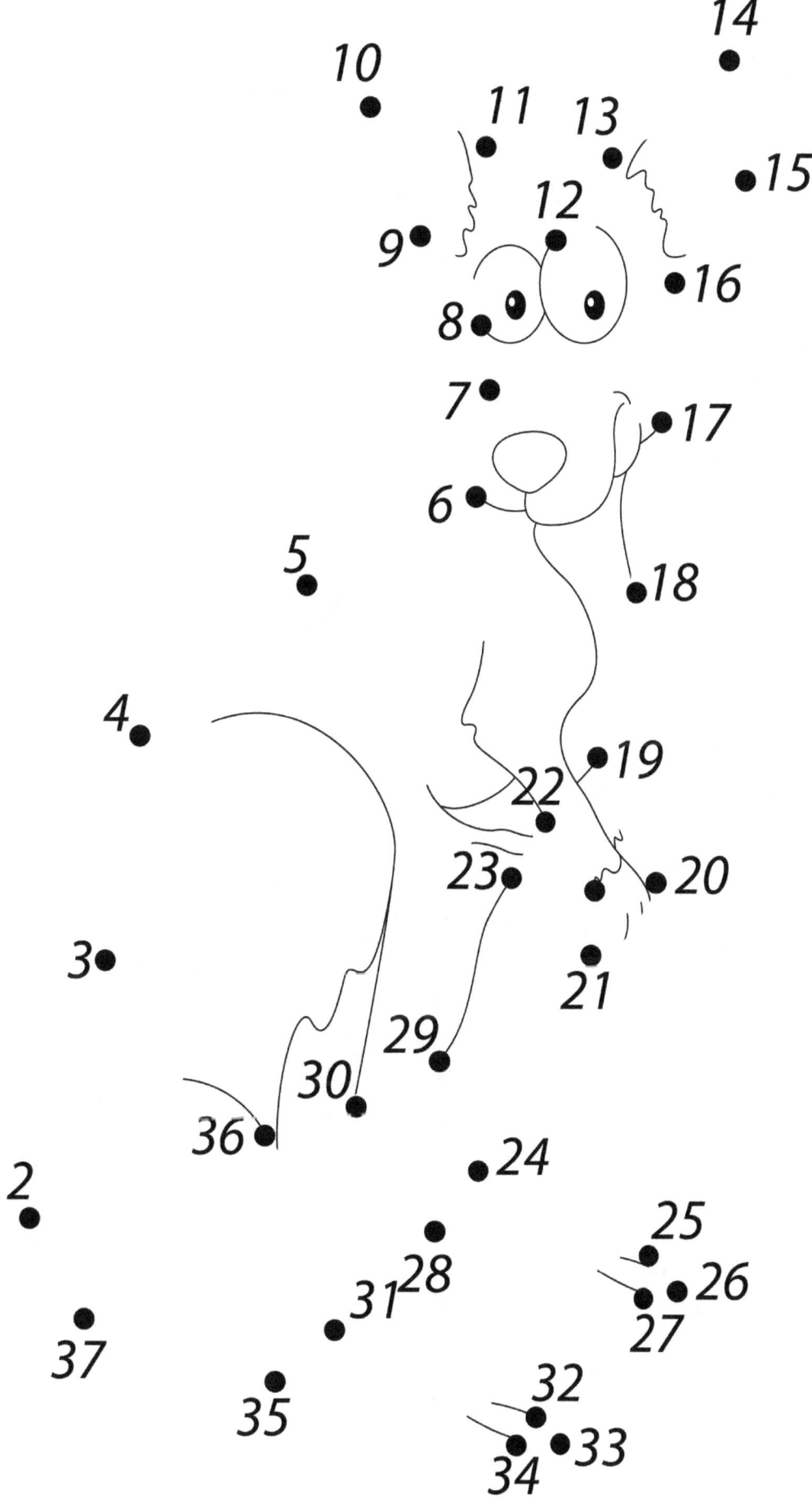

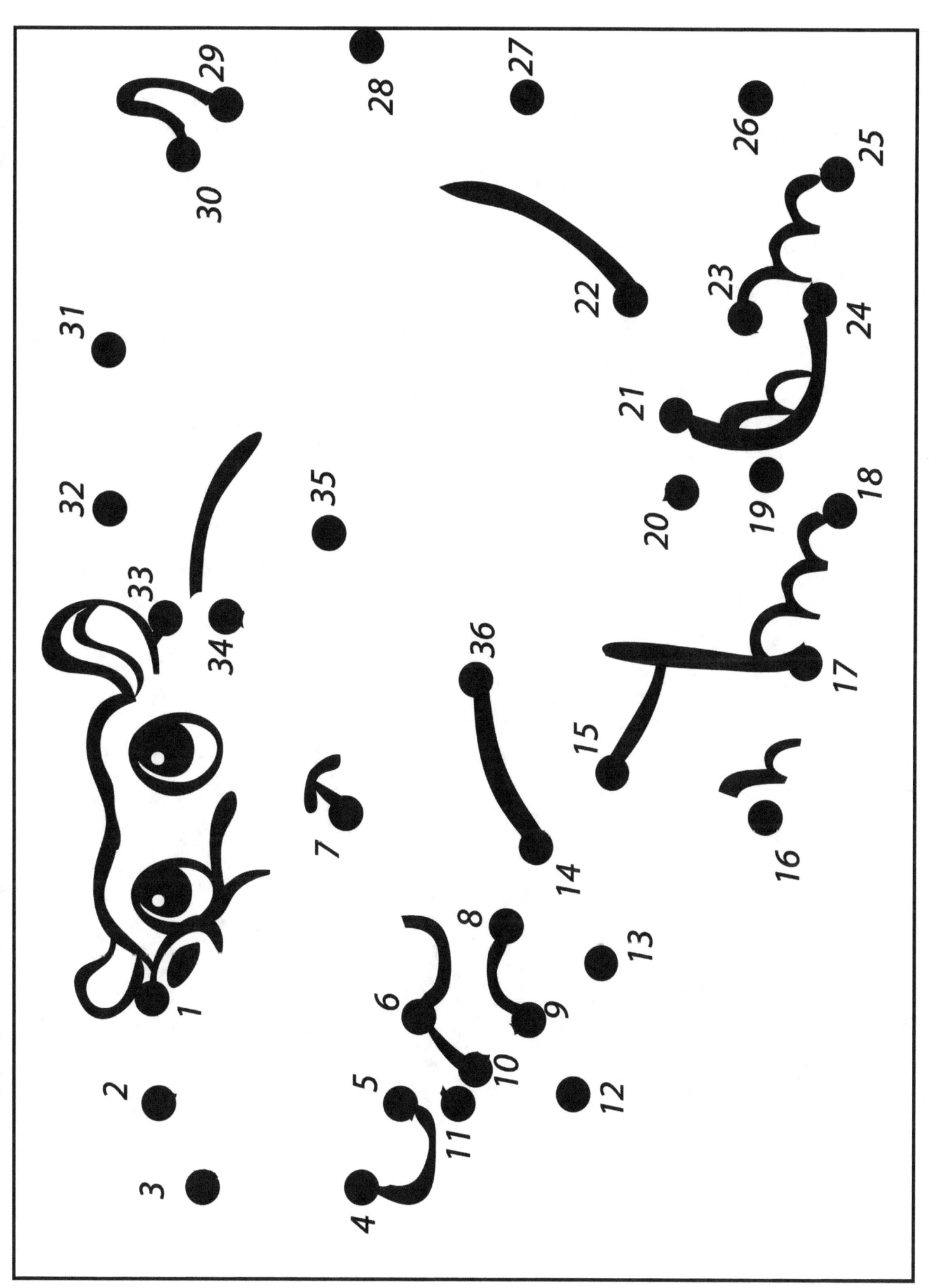

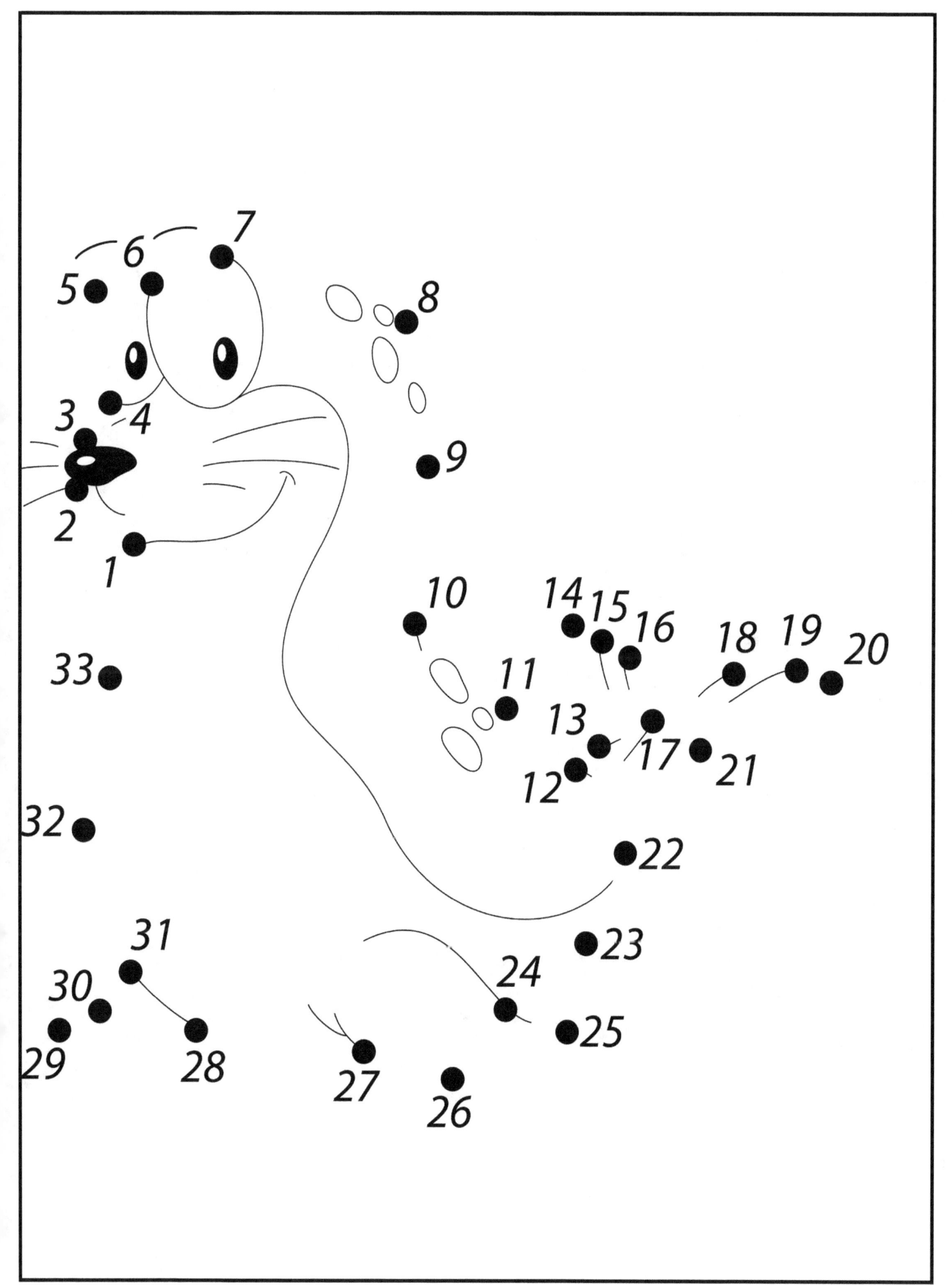

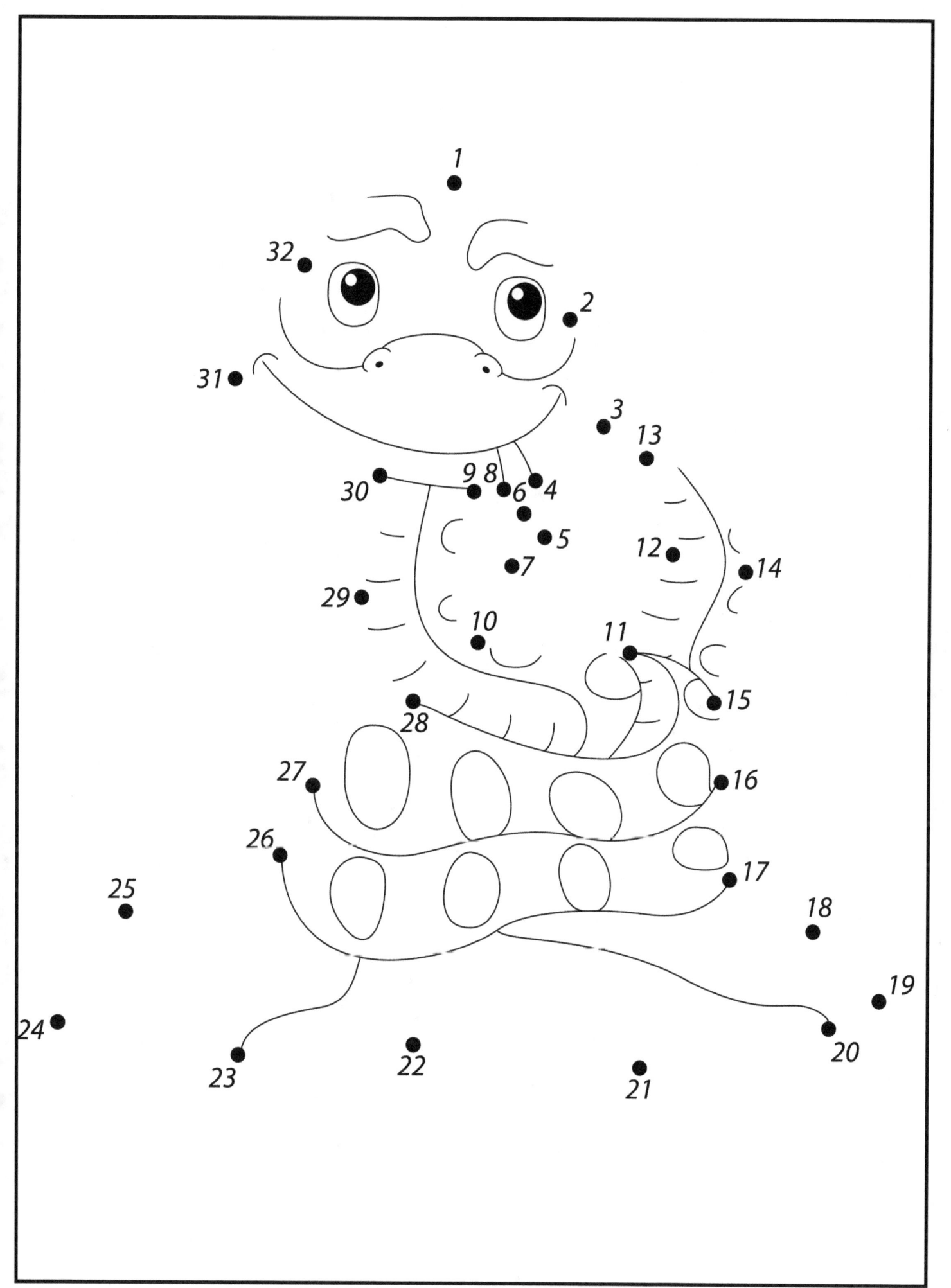

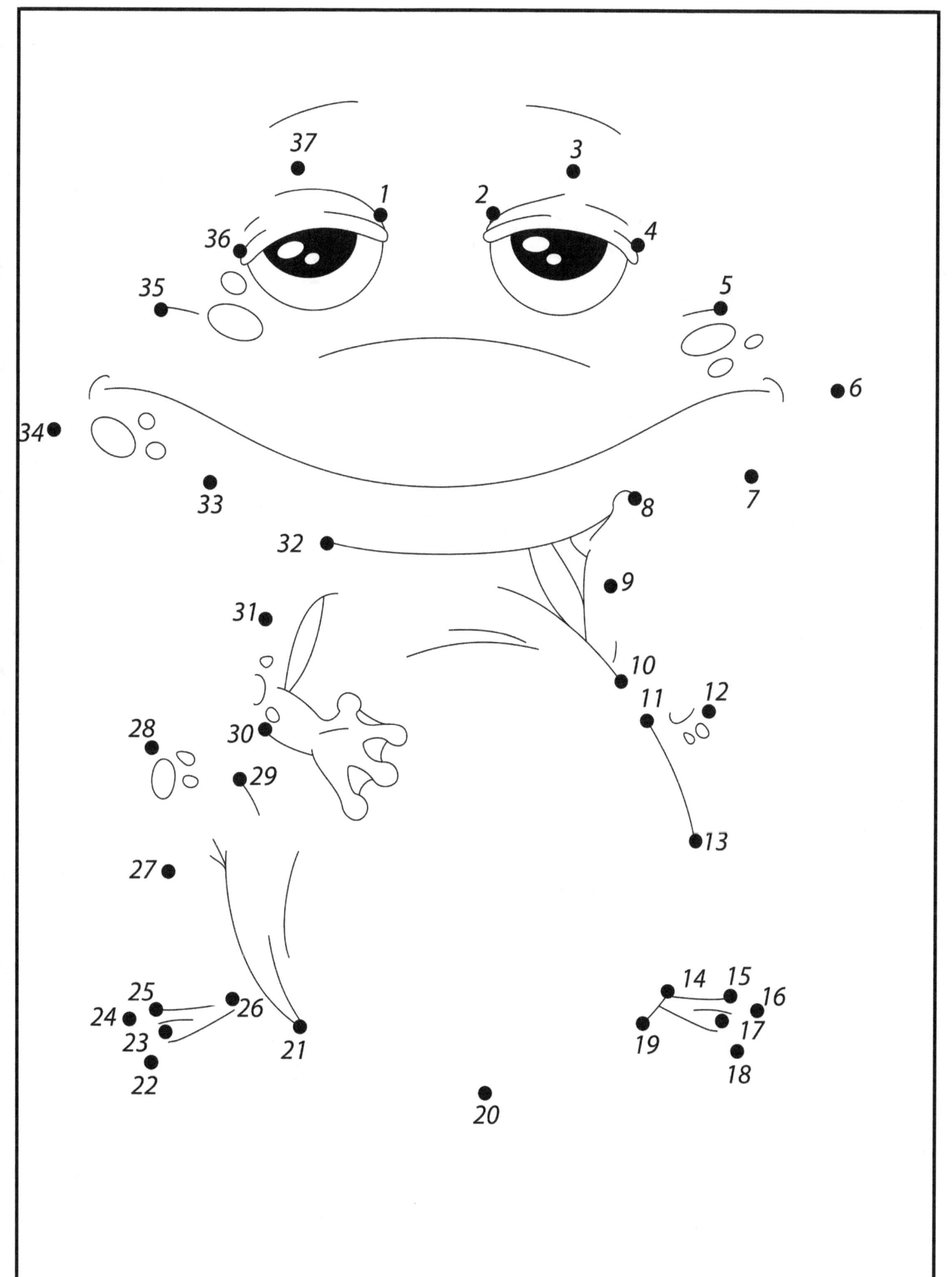

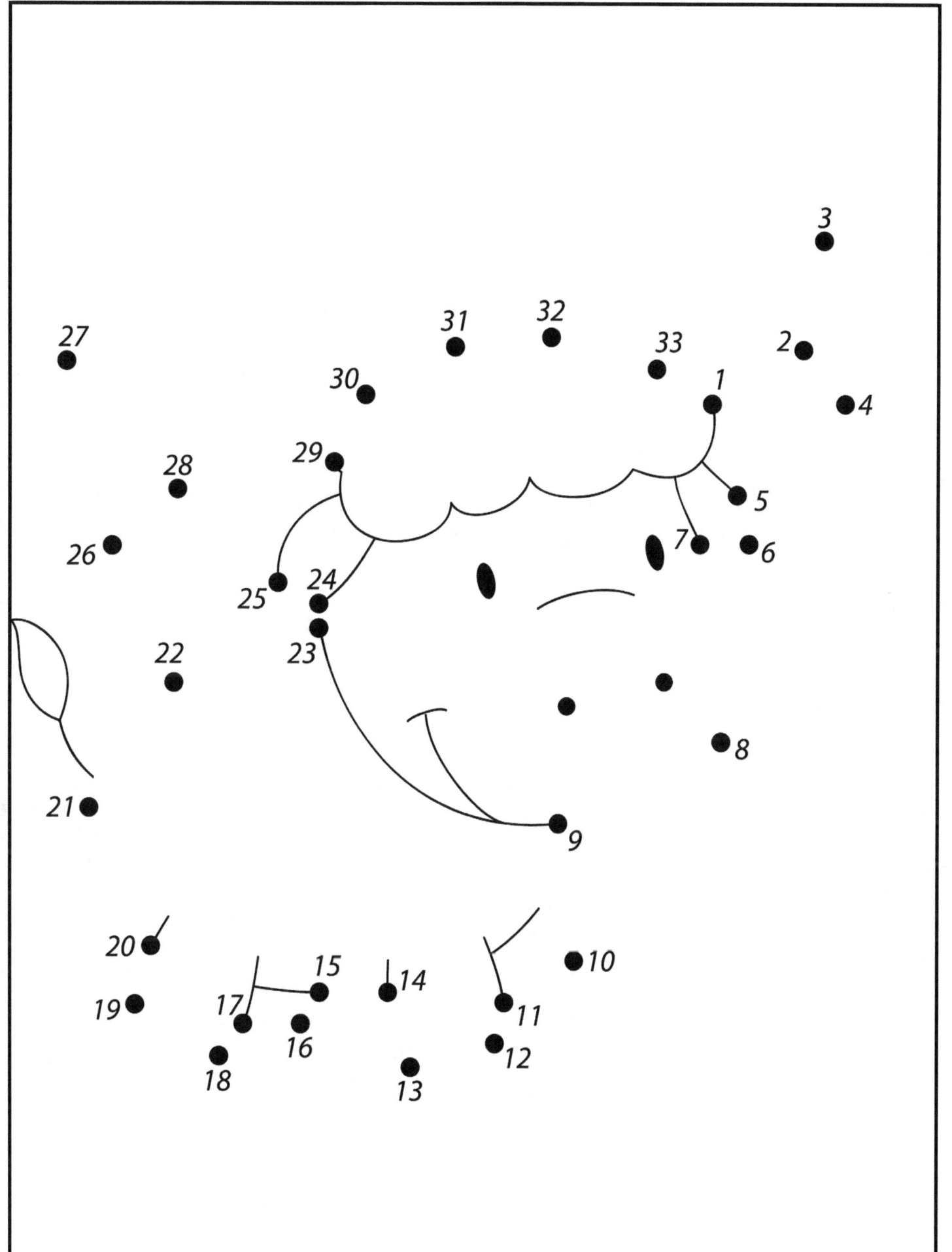

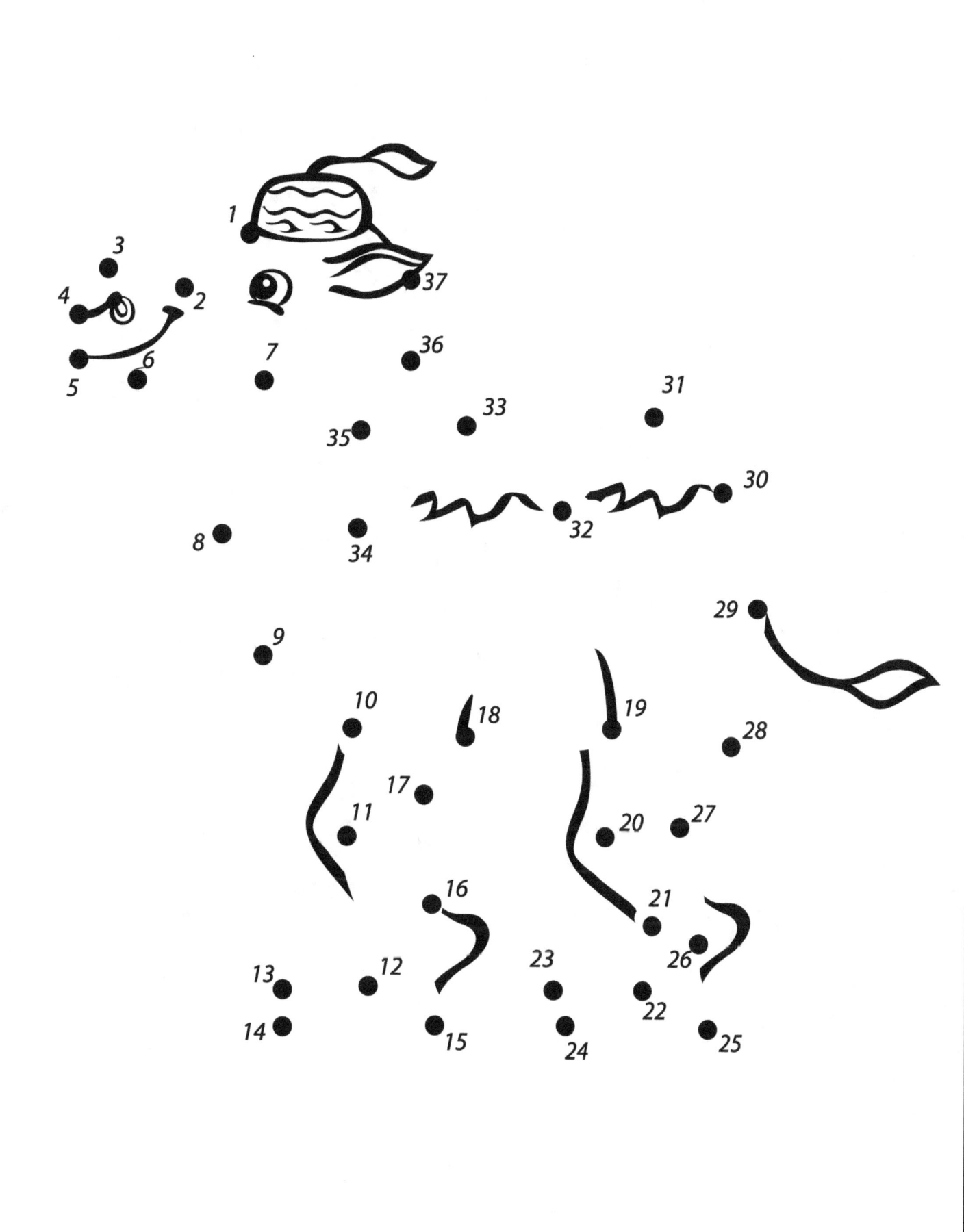

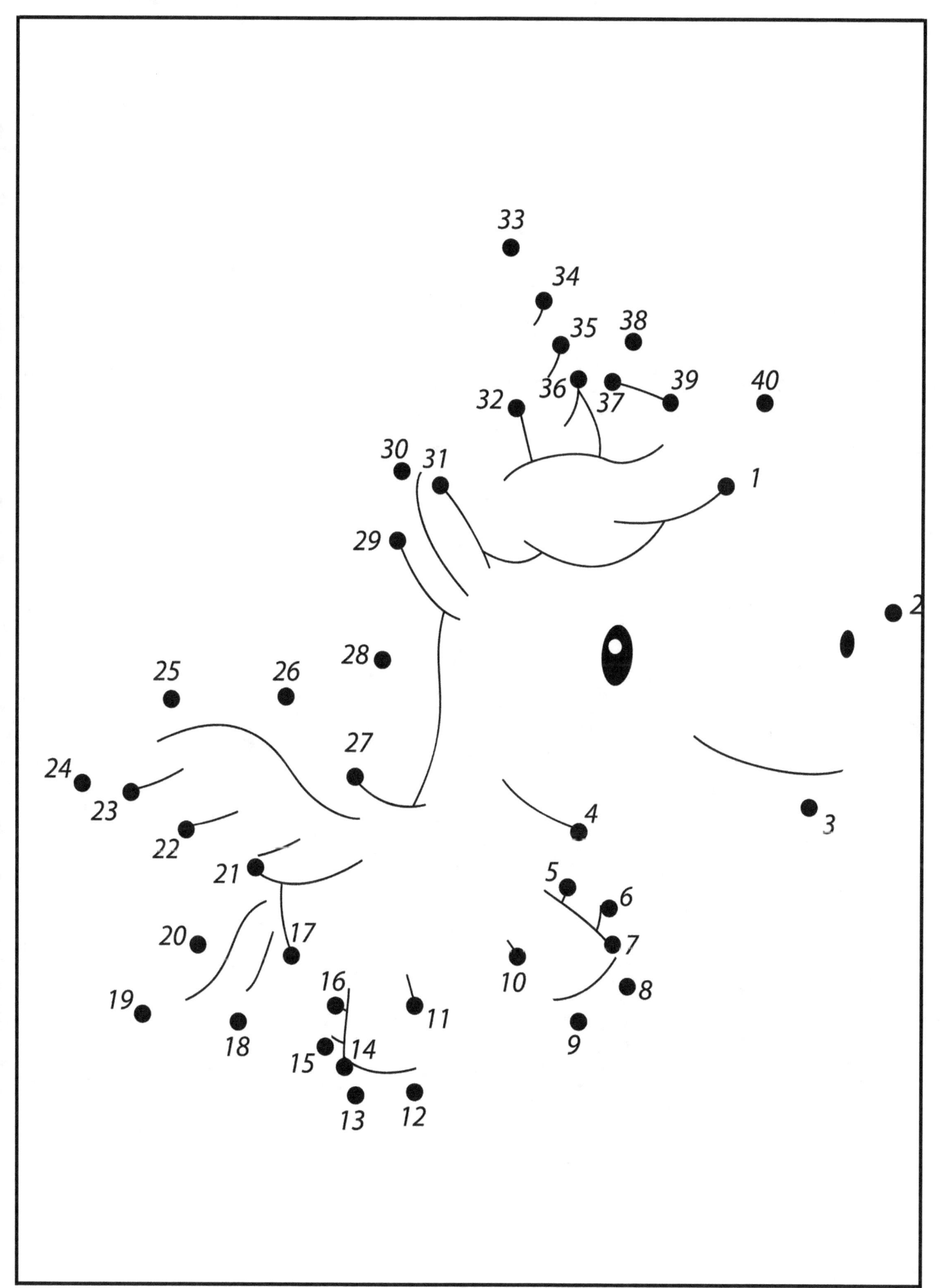

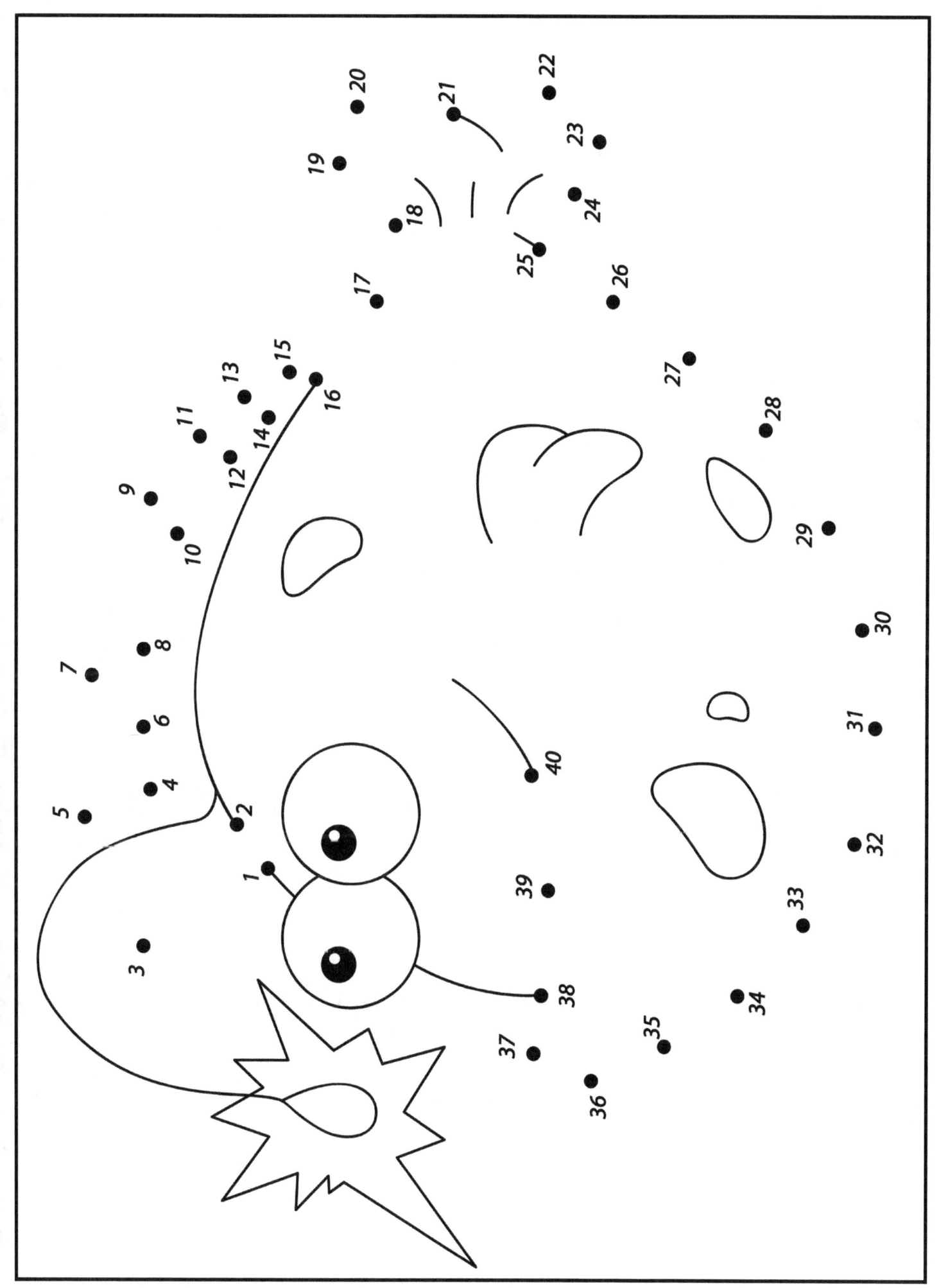

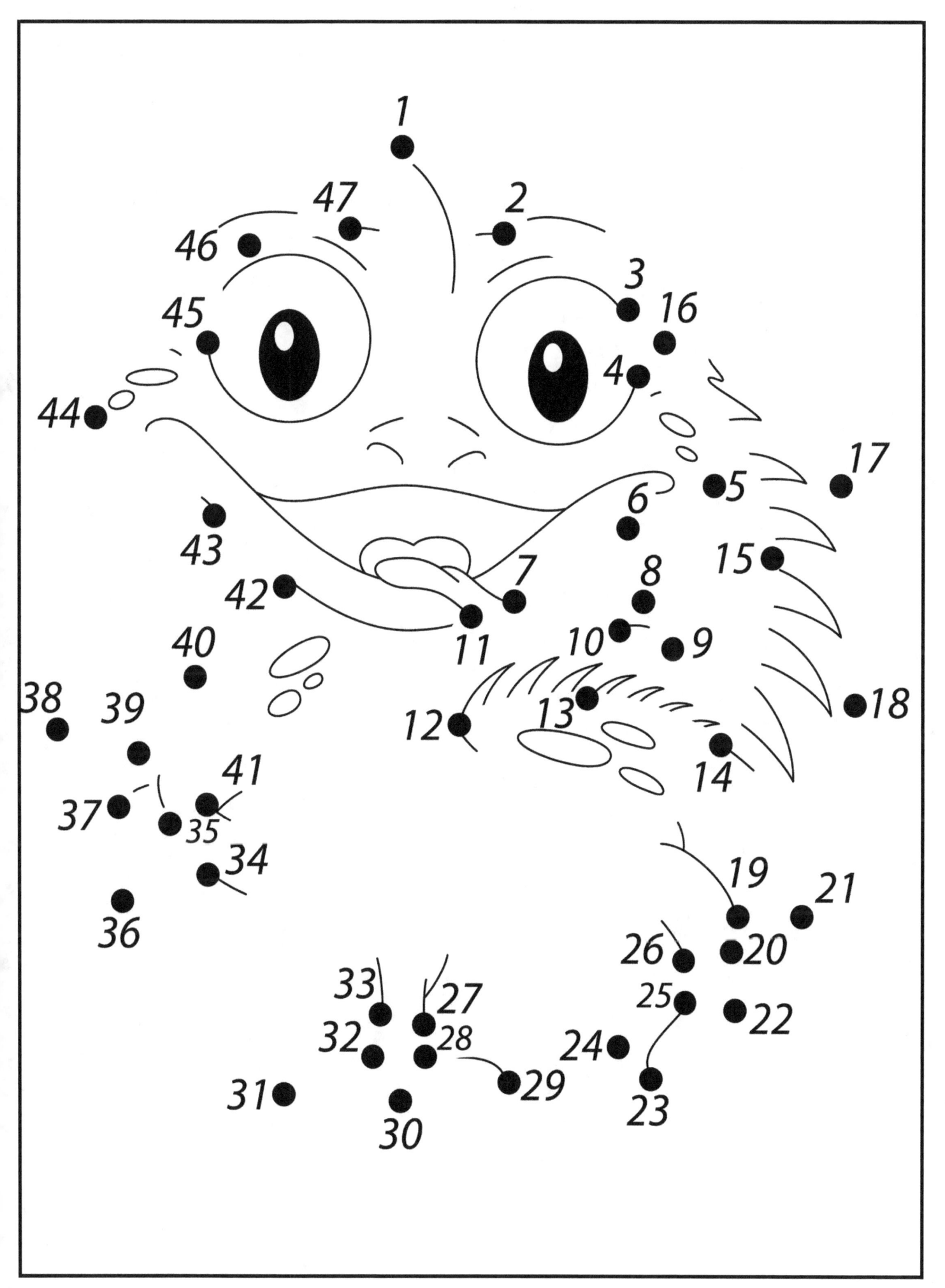

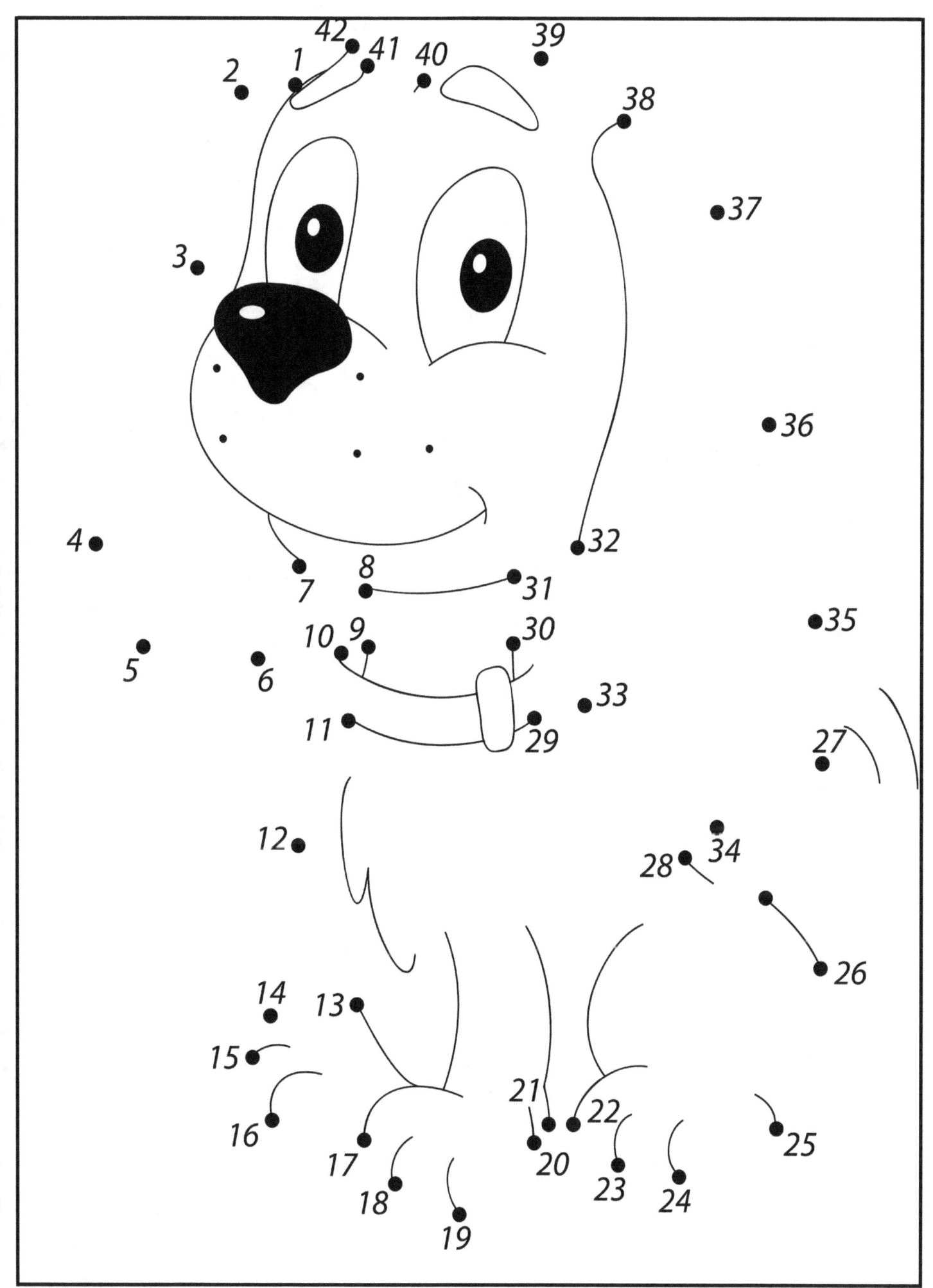

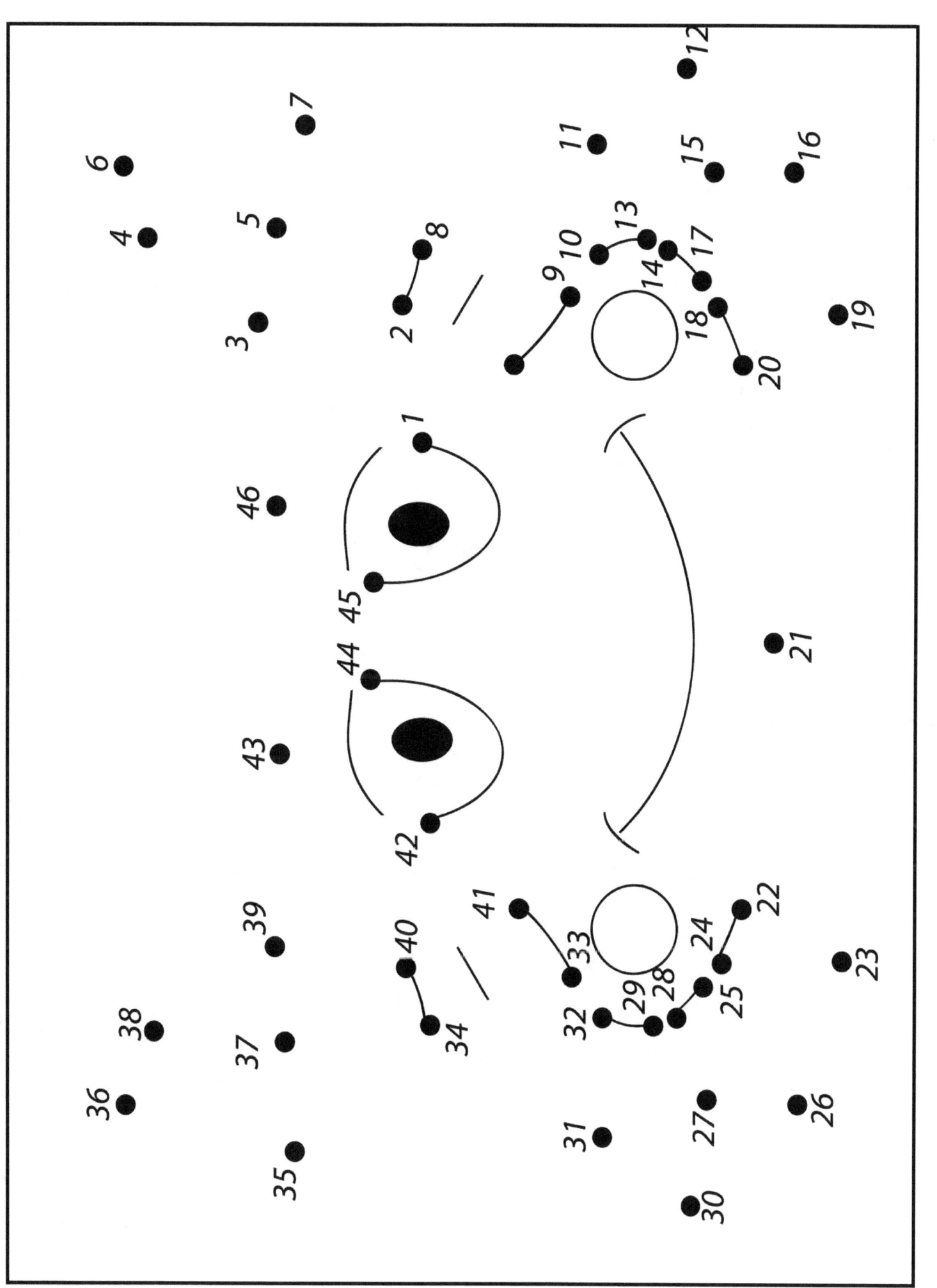

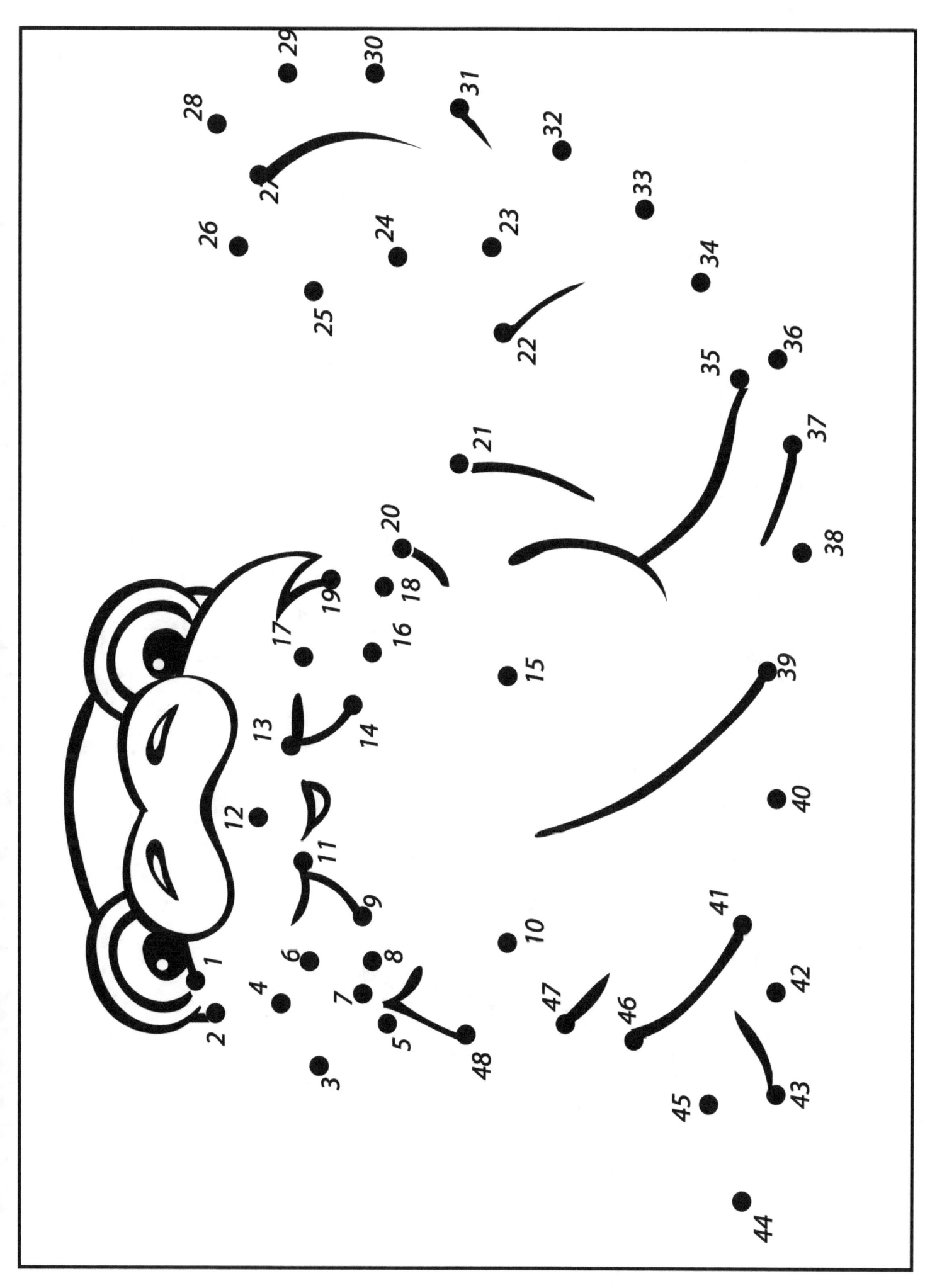

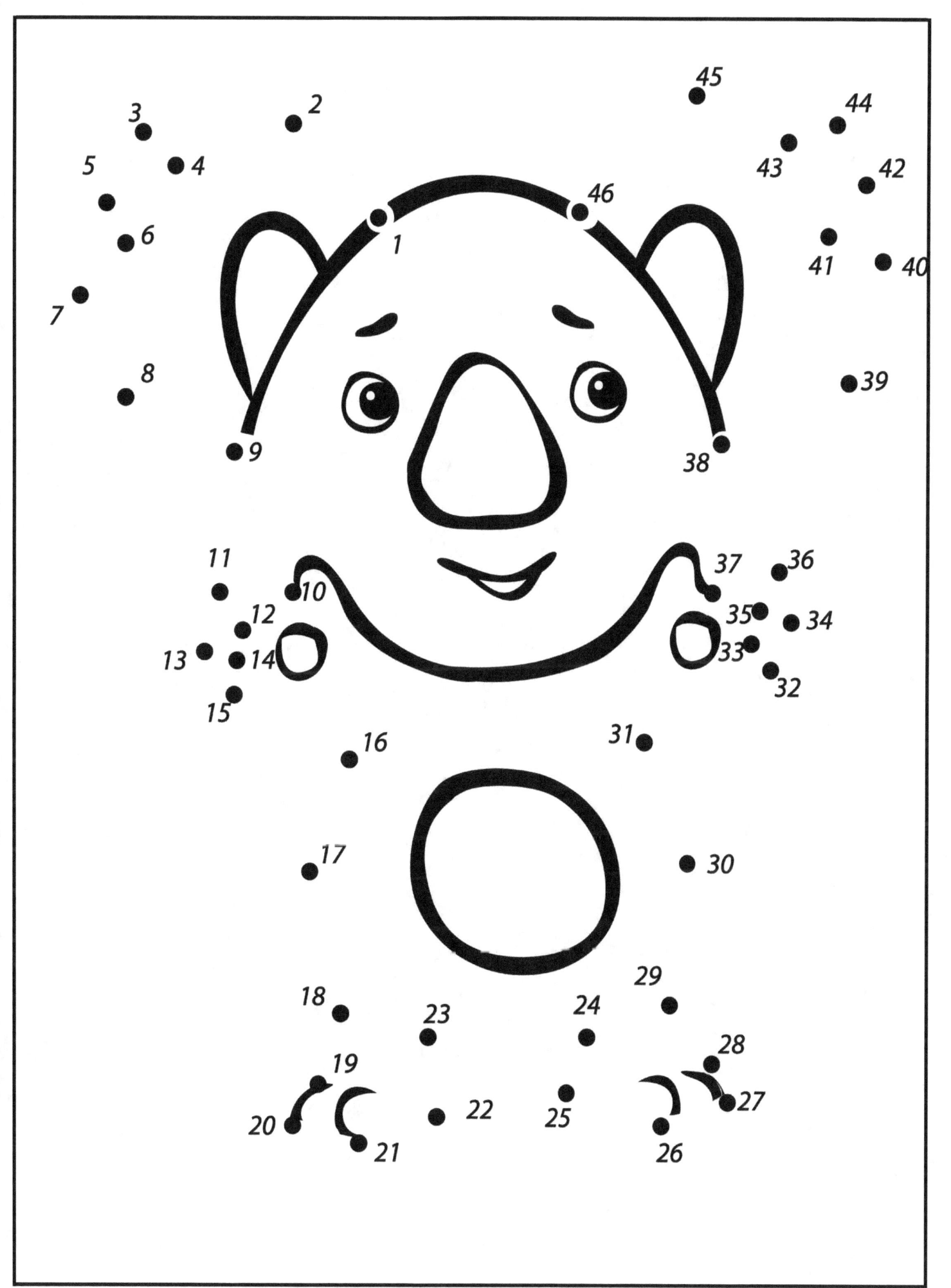

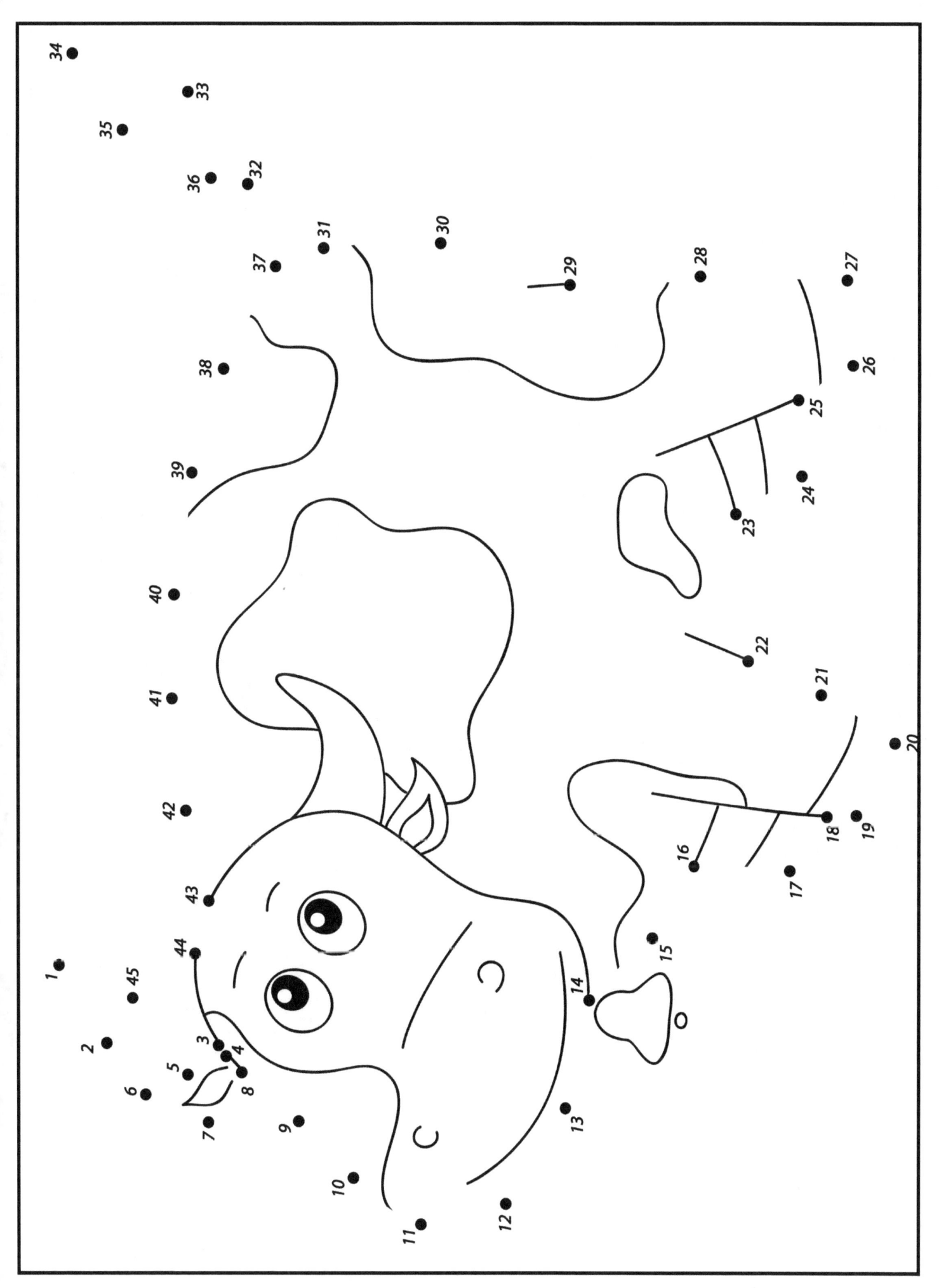

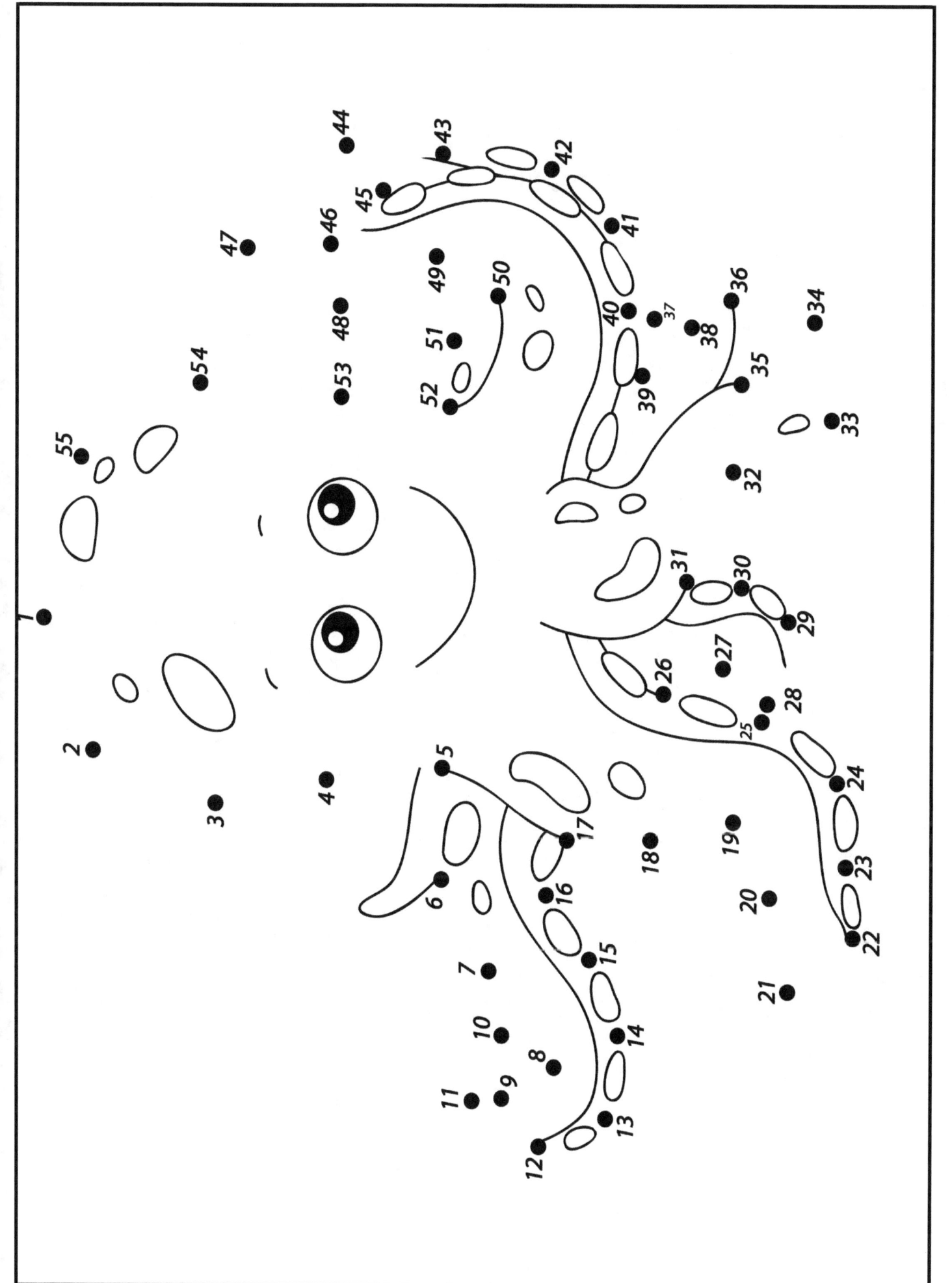

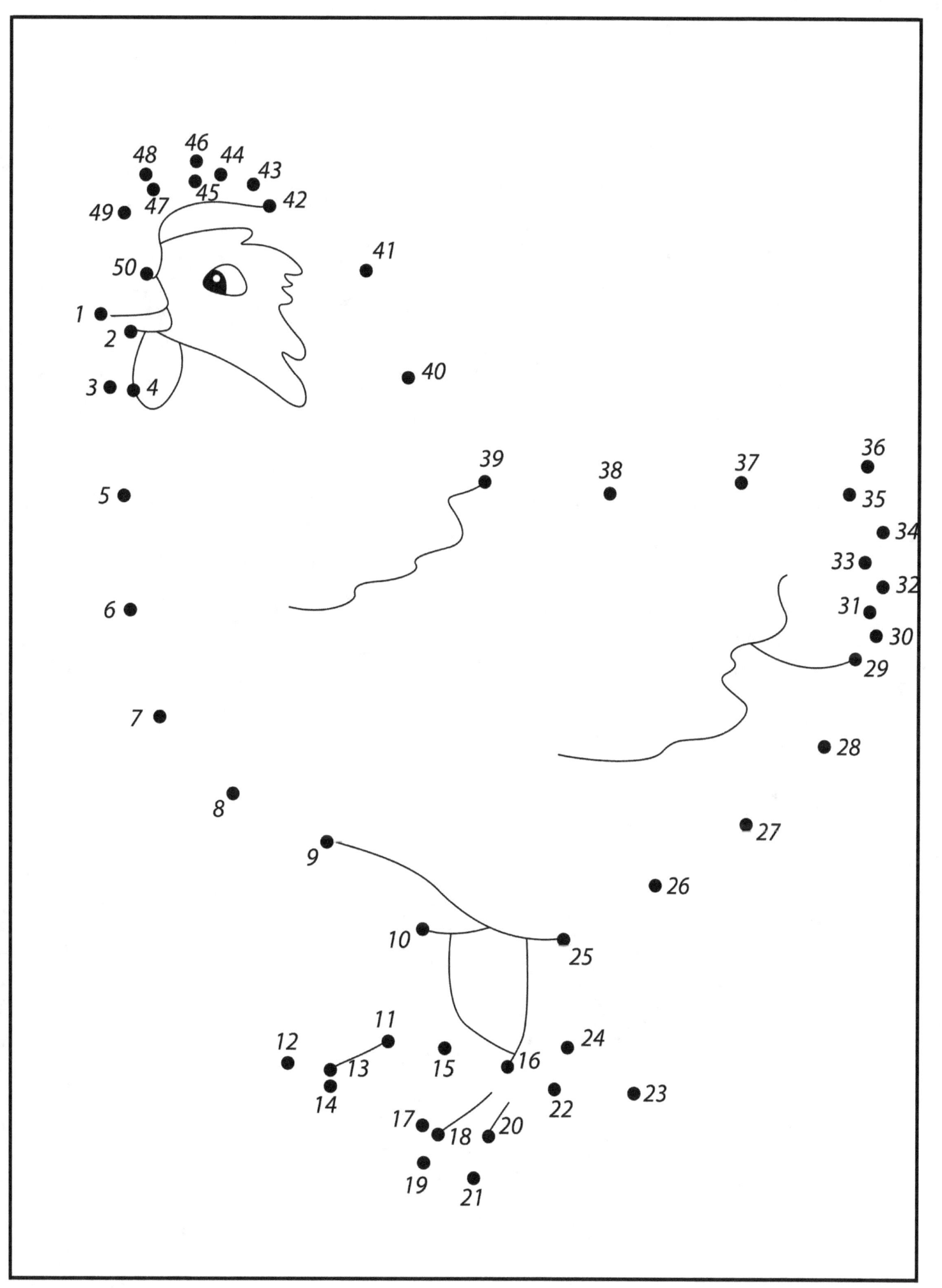

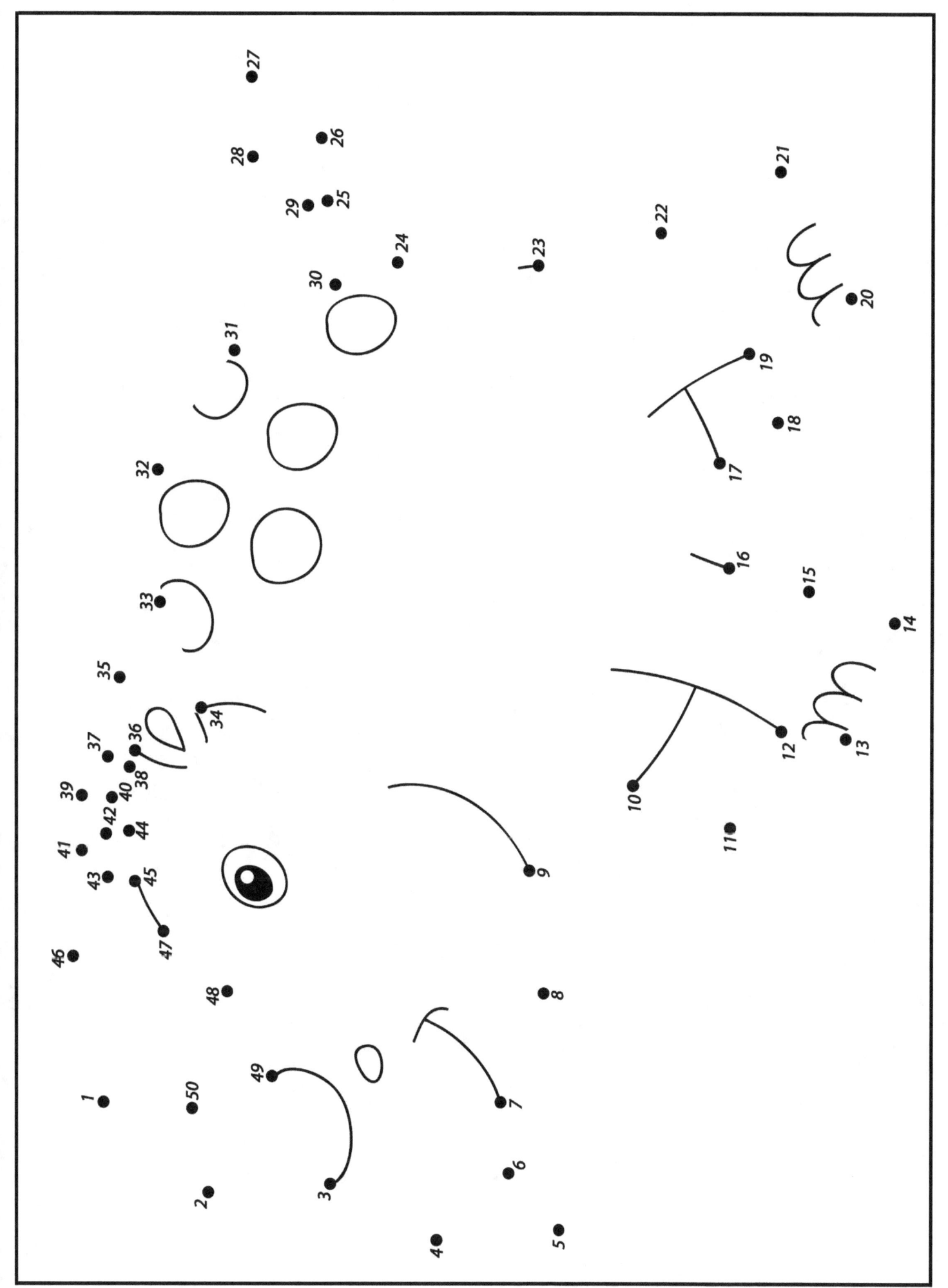

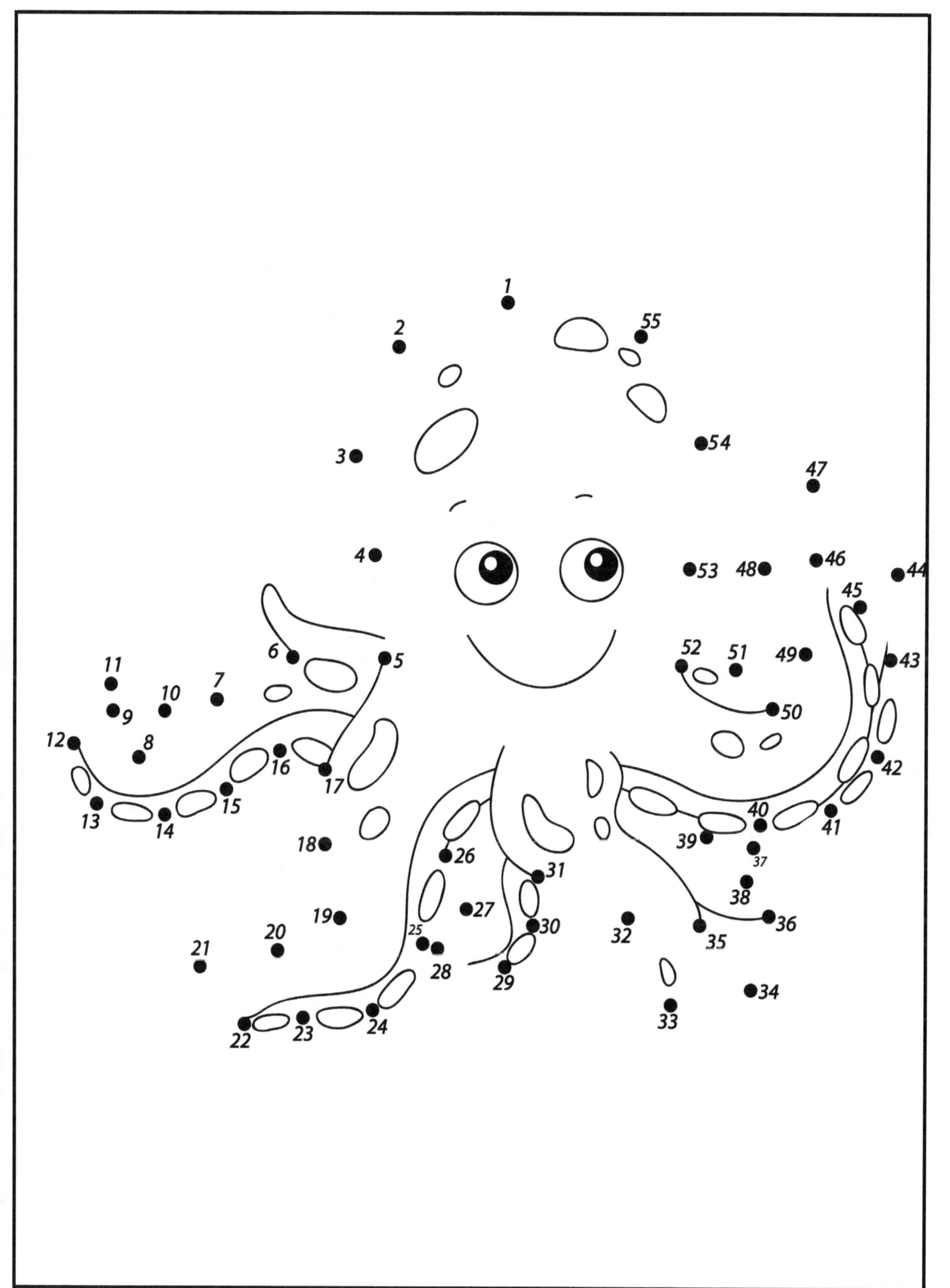

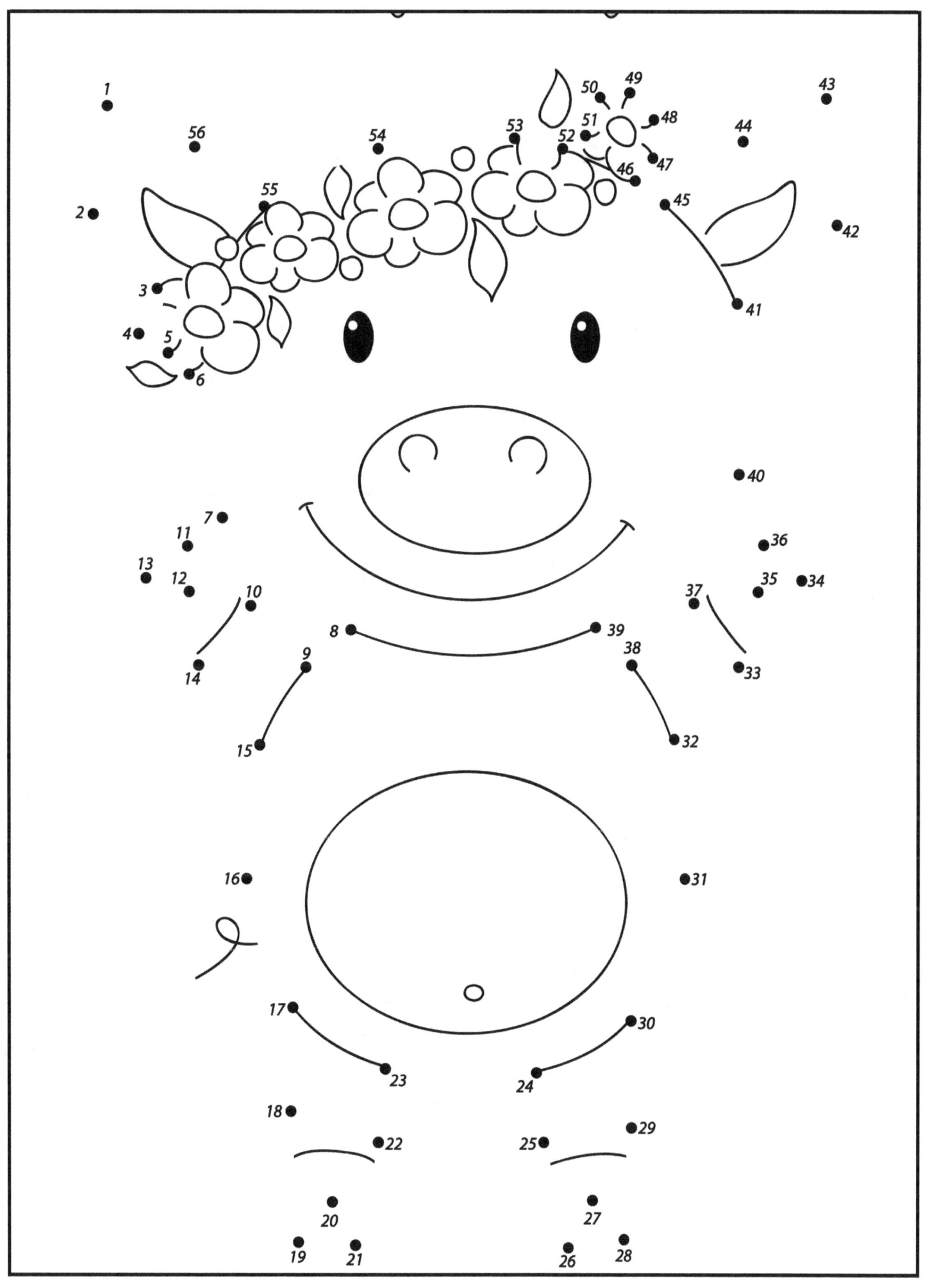

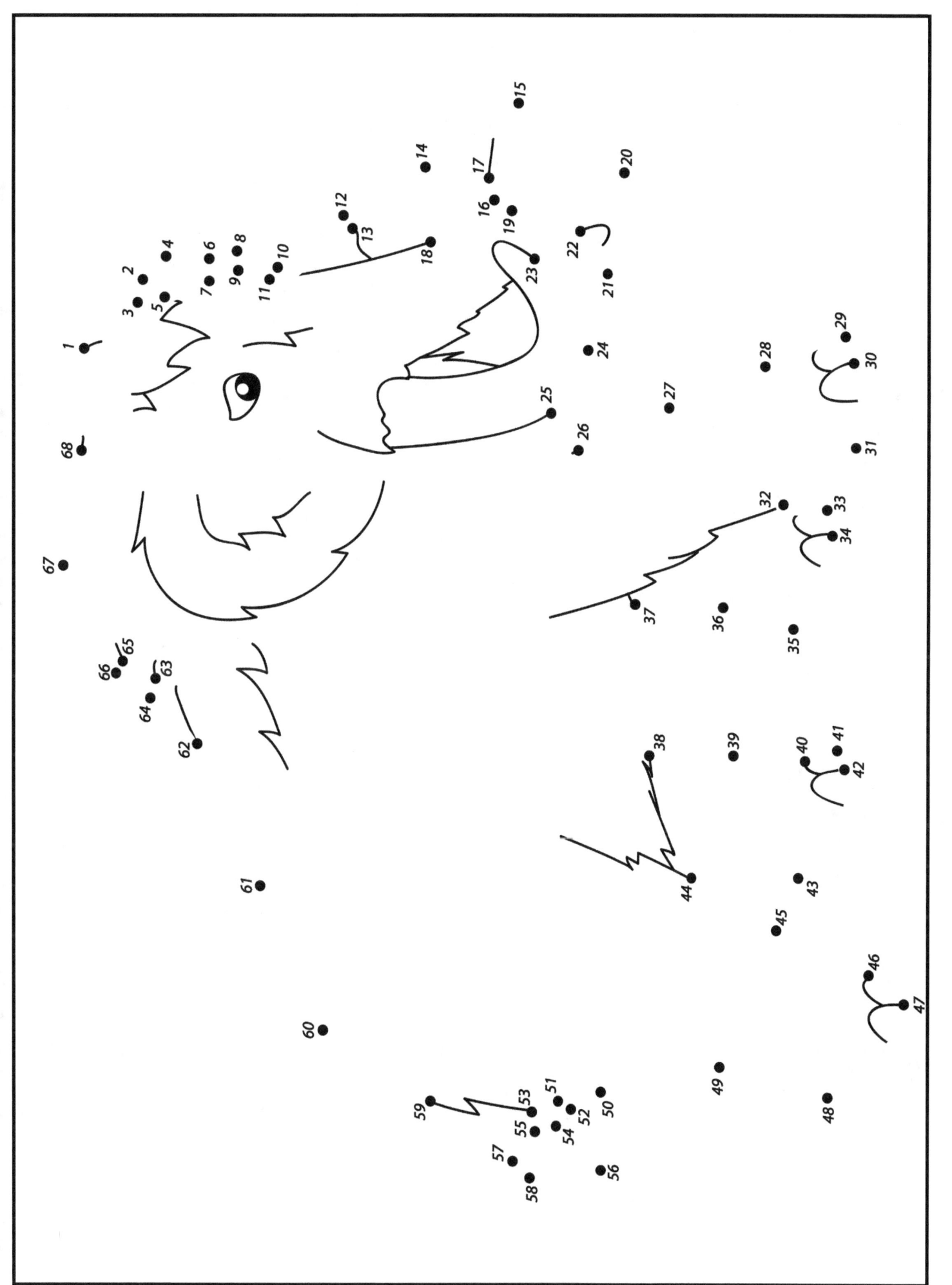

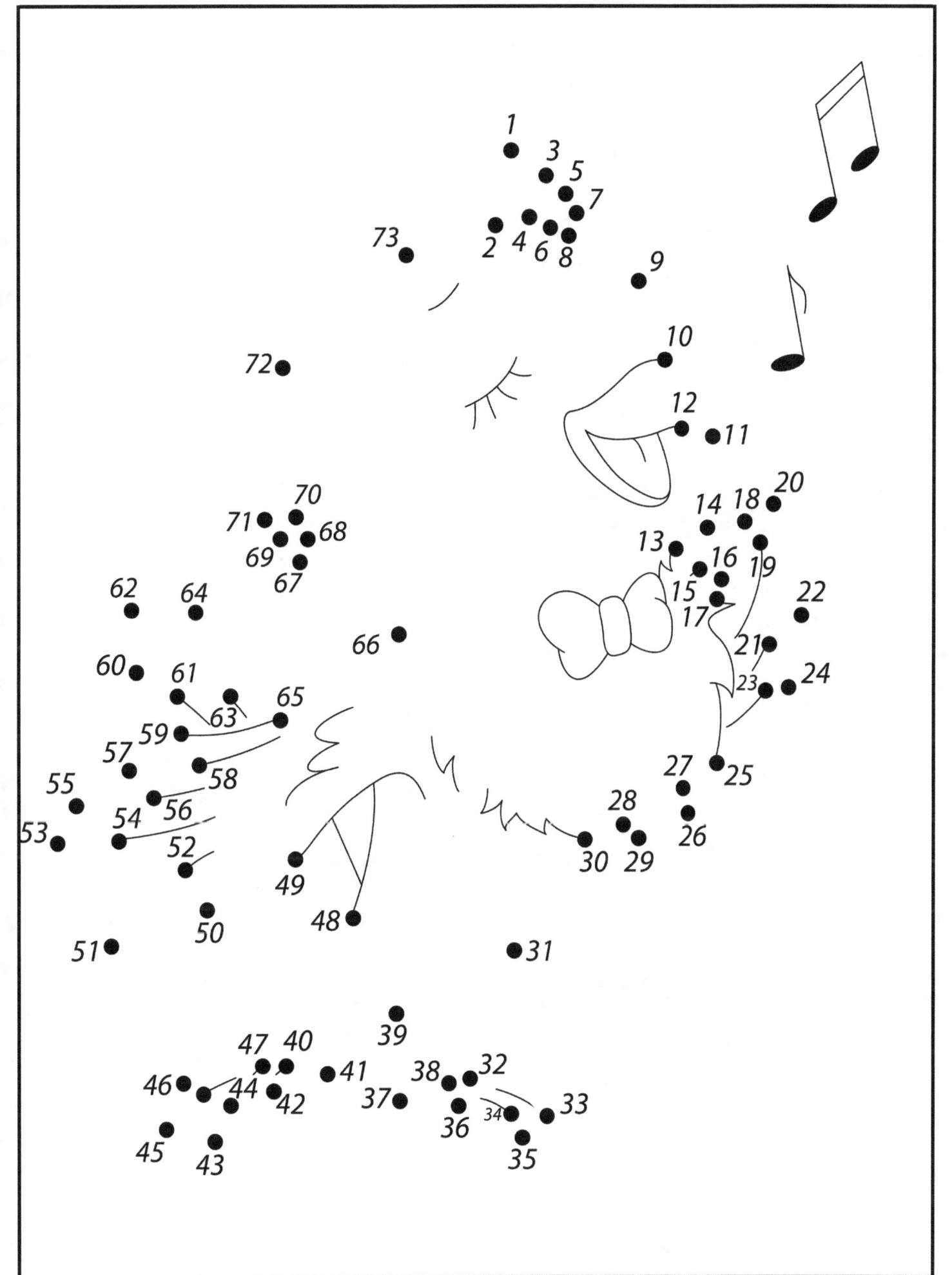

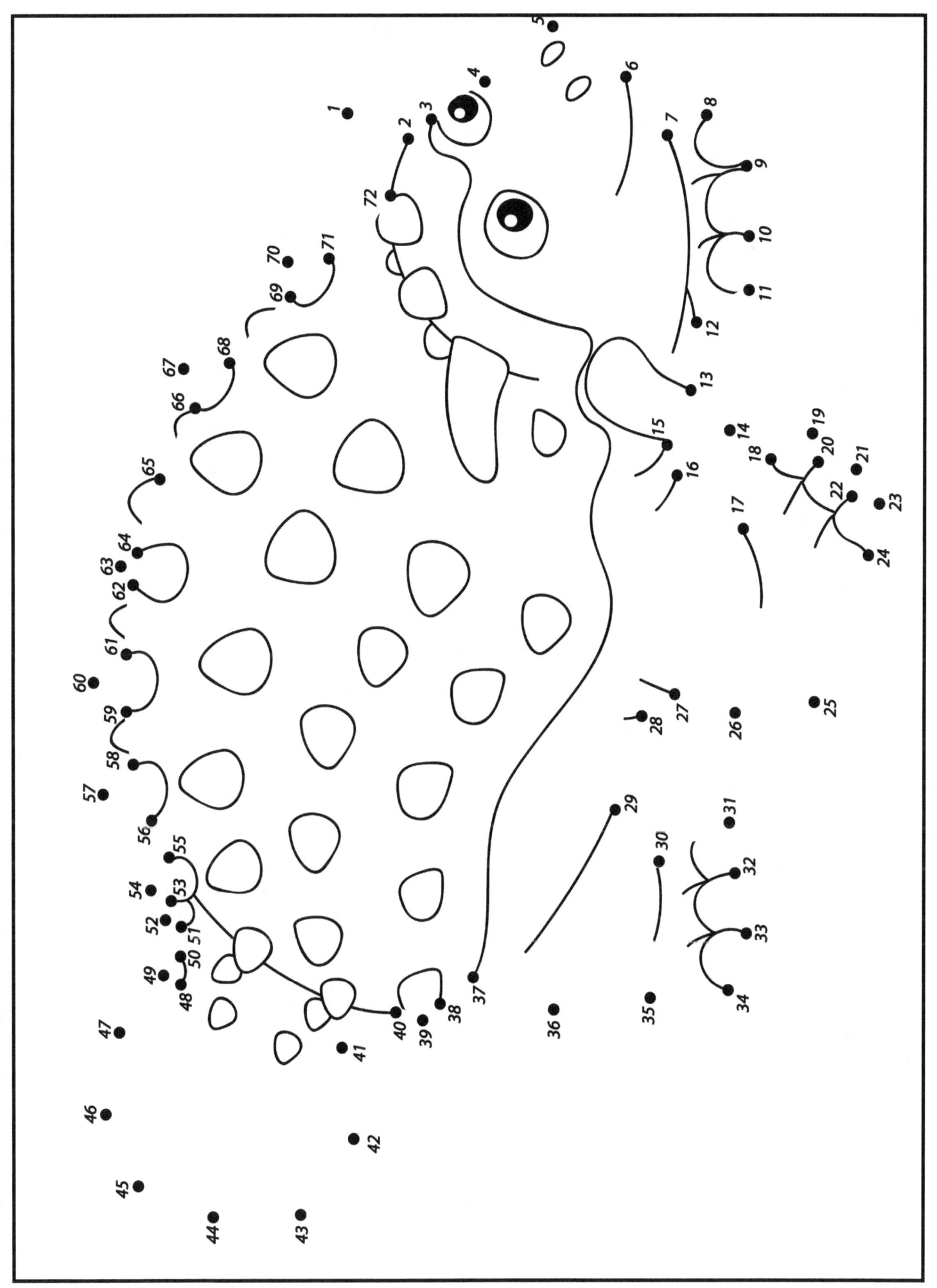

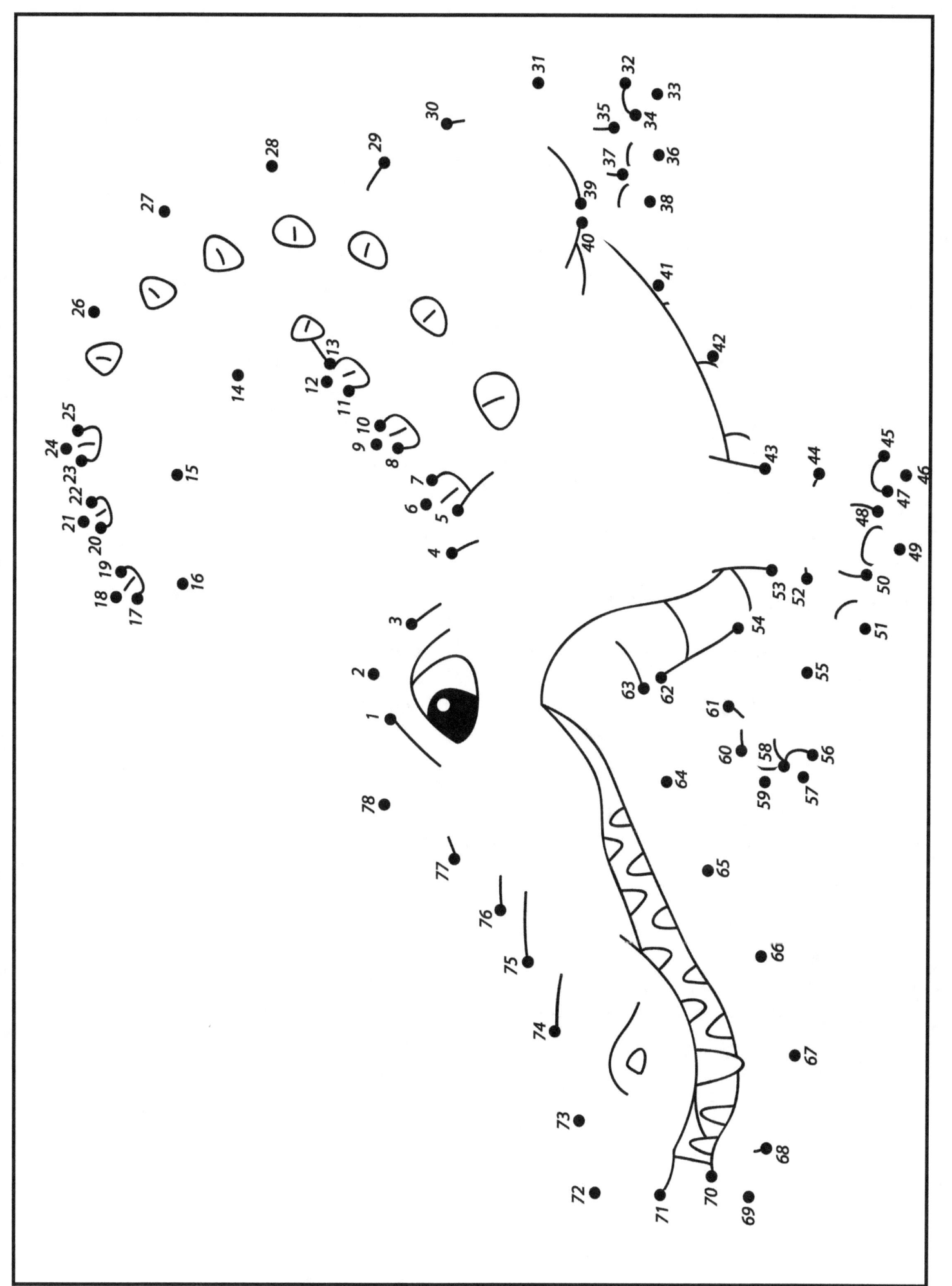

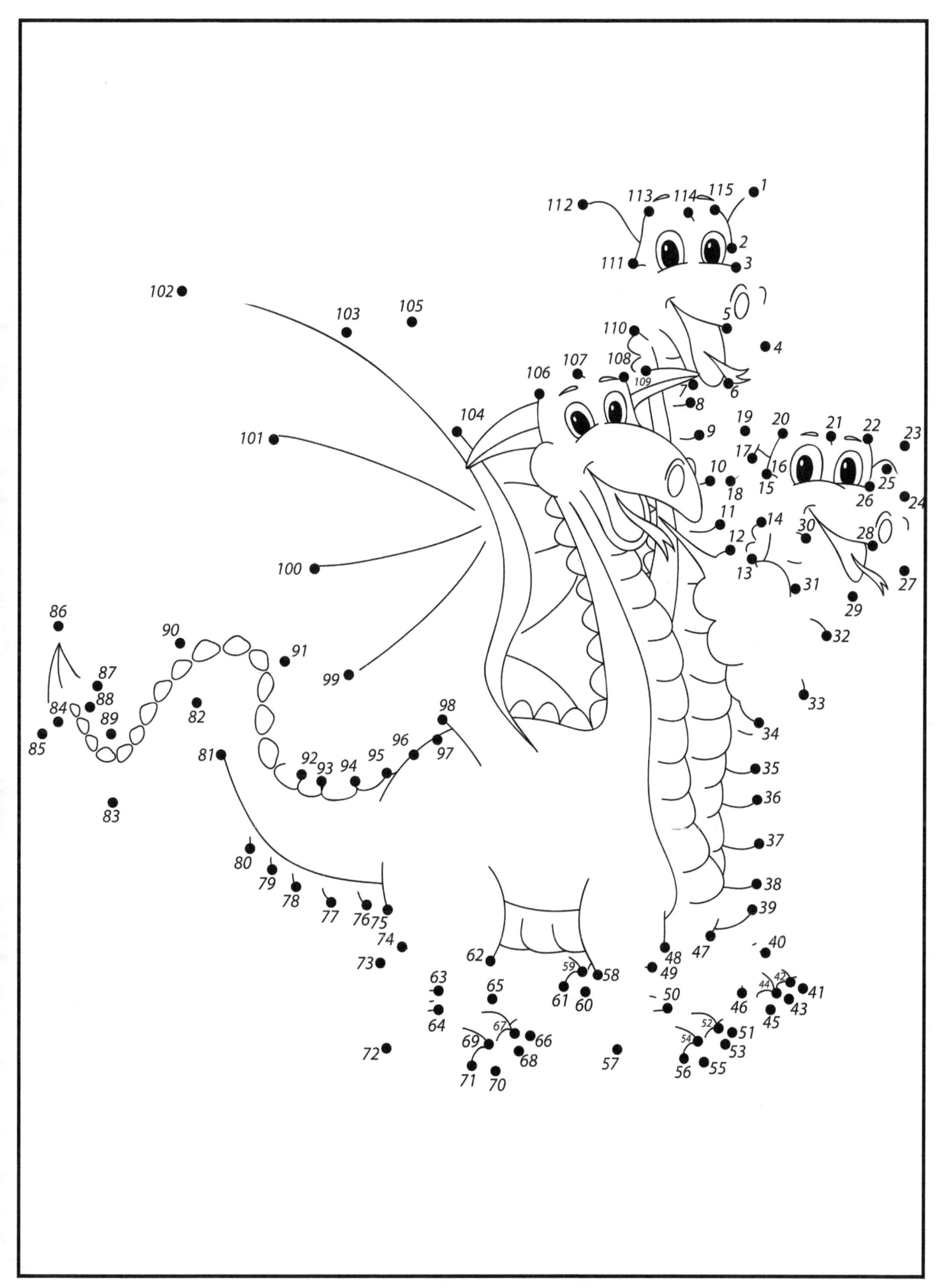

www.ingramcontent.com/pod-product-compliance
Lightning Source LLC
Chambersburg PA
CBHW080026130526
44591CB00037B/2678